LC
POC

GW00373012

1 LONDON GUIDE

Getting About *3*;
Entertainment for free *4*; Seeing the Sights *5*;
Museums and Galleries *6*; When the Sun Shines *7*; Taking
to the River *8*; Cultural Entertainment *9*; Rock, Pop and All
That Jazz *10*; Strictly for the Energetic *11*; Sinister London *12*;
Shopping Around *13*; Going to Market *14*; Eating and
Drinking *14*; Pubs *16*.

2 CENTRAL LONDON

Underground
map, *17*. Large scale maps showing the areas adjacent
to Piccadilly Circus, *18*. Theatres & cinemas map, *26*.

3 LONDON

Key map, *28*. Detailed maps
covering inner London between Regent's Park and the
Oval and from Kensington to the London Docks, *30*. Shopping
map, *64*.

4 STREET INDEX

Over 4,000 street
names from both map sections are listed in
the index, *65*.

GEOGRAPHIA

ROBERT NICHOLSON PUBLICATIONS

Map references
The letters A or B precede the map page number and indicate
whether the street is to be found in the upper half of the page
(A), or (B) the lower half.

First published 1981

2nd edition 1984

3rd edition 1985

© Text, **Robert Nicholson Publications Limited 1986**

Central London and London Maps
© **Geographia Limited**
based upon the Ordnance Survey with the sanction of the
controller of Her Majesty's Stationery Office.
Crown Copyright reserved.

London Underground map by
kind permission of London Transport.
Registered User Number 85/067

All other maps
© Robert Nicholson Publications Limited

Robert Nicholson Publications Limited
62–65 Chandos Place
London WC2N 4NW

Great care has been taken throughout this book to be accurate,
but the publishers cannot accept responsibility for any errors
which appear or their consequences.

Typeset by The Castlefield Press
Northampton

Printed in the United Kingdom by
Chorley & Pickersgill Limited, Leeds

First, some basic information about money. For cash, banks offer the best rate of exchange (*open 09.30–15.30 Mon to Fri, closed Bank hols*). Some department stores have bureaux de change, most hotels will cash traveller's cheques.

London Guide *1*

GETTING ABOUT

TOURIST INFORMATION
City of London Information Centre B43
St Paul's Churchyard Ec4, 01-606 3030. All about the City. *Diary of Events* lists free entertainment.
National Tourist Information Centre A59
Main forecourt, Victoria Station SW1. Multi-lingual tourist and travel information. Also instant hotel reservations, theatre and tour bookings. Bookshop. *Open 09.00–20.30, 08.30–22.00 Jul & Aug.* Telephone information service: 01-730 3488.
Harrods, Knightsbridge SW1 B48
Heathrow Central Underground Station
Selfridges, Oxford St W1 B38
Tower of London, West Gate E1 A55

TRAVEL
Underground trains and buses usually stop between *24.00 and 06.00.* However, there are some all-night buses and if you are planning a late night out in town, consult 'The Night Owl's Guide' available from London Transport Information Centre or telephone 01-222 1234 at any time. All underground stations have a notice of first and last trains. Some bus stops list first and last buses.
London Transport Travel Information Centres
For enquiries on tube and bus travel, sight-seeing tours and special cut-price touring tickets:
Euston Underground Station B33
Heathrow Central Underground Station
King's Cross Underground Station A34
Oxford Circus Underground Station B40
Piccadilly Circus Underground Station A50
Victoria Underground Station A59

ENTERTAINMENT FOR FREE

How to spend a pleasant hour or so without spending money. Here are some famous London attractions.

CHANGING OF THE GUARD
Telephone London Tourist Board (01-730 3488) for details.

Buckingham Palace B49
SW1. New guard marches from Chelsea or Wellington Barracks; changes *11.30 daily, alt days in winter.*

Horseguards Parade B51
Whitehall SW1. Queen's Life Guard, on great black horses, leave Hyde Park Barracks *10.38 Mon-Sat, 09.39 Sun.* Ceremony *11.00 Mon-Sat, 10.00 Sun.*

CHURCH CONCERTS
Free lunchtime concerts, though there is usually a collection.

St Bride B42
Fleet St EC4. 01-353 1301. *Wed.*

St Martin-in-the-Fields A51
Trafalgar Sq WC2. 01-930 0089. *Mon & Tue.*

St John's A61
Smith Square SW1. 01-222 1061. *Mon & alt Thur.*

HOUSES OF PARLIAMENT A61
St Margaret St SW1. 01-219 3000. Look around the Victorian-Gothic pile (built 1840–68 by Sir Charles Barry and A. W. N. Pugin) when Parliament is in recess. (Permission from your MP or through your embassy is necessary.) Or queue for admission during debates. Be sure to admire the famous clock tower, 'Big Ben'.

MILITARY AND BRASS BANDS
For rousing British music go to a public park on a summer afternoon. Check *What's On & Where to Go* for details. Try:

Lincoln's Inn Fields B42
WC2. *Tue & Thur in summer.*

St James's Park B50
SW1. *Every lunchtime and early eve. Mon-Fri, Sun & B. hols.*

Regent's Park A32
NW1. *Every lunchtime and early eve Mon-Fri, Sun & B. hols.*

OLD BAILEY B43
Old Bailey EC4. 01-248 3277. Climb to the public gallery to watch criminals getting their come-uppance. *Mon-Fri.*

SPEAKER'S CORNER A48
Marble Arch corner of Hyde Park. Where unknown orators explain their views of life. Feel free to argue. *Sun.*

SEEING THE SIGHTS

Apart from the cost of getting there, seeing the sights is also free. Here are some of the most dramatic, most intriguing and most British of them.

Buckingham Palace   B49

St James's Pk SW1. London residence of the Sovereign (the Royal Standard flies when She is at home). Built 1705, remodelled by Nash, 1825, refaced by Sir Ashton Webb 1913.

The Cenotaph   B51

Whitehall SW1. Designed 1920 by Sir Edward Lutyens to honour the dead of World War I. Wreaths are laid here annually at the culmination of the Remembrance Day Service in memory of those who fell in both world wars.

City of London   B44

The 'square mile' of the City is the oldest part of London and the centre of banking, insurance and stockbroking. Look for sections of the Roman Wall, medieval streets and alleys, old taverns and churches that survived the Great Fire of 1666.

Covent Garden   B41

The former home of the famous fruit and vegetable market – today one of London's most popular meeting places. Grand Victorian warehouses shelter craft shops, gift stalls, wine bars, restaurants and art galleries. Originally designed by Inigo Jones in the 1630s.

Downing St   B51

17thC houses built by Sir George Downing. No 10 is the official residence of the Prime Minister, No 11 of the Chancellor of the Exchequer. Handy for the Houses of Parliament, the offices and Ministries of Whitehall.

Fleet St   B42

The street of communications and the law. Many national newspapers have their offices on or just off it. Watch the legal eagles at work and play.

Piccadilly Circus   B40

Six major streets meet at the fountain and statue of Eros (Gilbert 1892). Not the glamorous meeting place it once was, but its fame lingers on. The young crowd permanently camped around the statue is still very much of today.

St Paul's Cathedral   B43

EC1. 01-248 4619/2705. Built by Christopher Wren from 1675–1710, and considered his greatest work. Superb dome, porches and monuments. The setting in 1981 for the marriage of Charles, Prince of Wales and Lady Diana Spencer.

Soho   B40

London's oldest 'foreign quarter', encompassing the whole of Chinatown. Plenty of foreign restaurants, also a certain amount of sex in the form of strip shows, blue movies, 'young models' and so on. But a 'clean-up' campaign is under way.

The Temple A52
Inner Temple, Crown Office Row EC4. 01-353 8462. Middle
Temple, Middle Temple La EC4. 01-353 4355. Two Inns of Court.
Wander round the courtyards, alleys, gardens and the early Gothic
'round' church built by the Templars. *At weekends & B. hols* enter
via Embankment.

Trafalgar Square A51
Nelson's column (1840) guarded by Landseer's bronze lions.
Meeting place for political demonstrators and pigeons.

Westminster Abbey A61
(The Collegiate Church of St Peter in Westminster) Broad
Sanctuary SW1. 01-222 5152. Original church by Edward the
Confessor, 1065. Rebuilt by Henry III from 1245 and completed
1376–1506. Fine perpendicular with fan vaulting. Contains
Coronation Chair, tombs and memorials of the Royalty of England
and their subjects.

MUSEUMS AND GALLERIES

When it rains, here are some interesting and stimulating shelters,
all free unless indicated.

British Museum A41
Gt Russell St WC1. 01-636 1555. One of the largest and greatest in
the world – Egyptian mummies, Assyrian bulls, Elgin Marbles,
Rosetta Stone. *Closed Sun morn.*

Hayward Gallery B52
Belvedere Rd SE1. 01-928 3144. Riverside gallery housing major
art exhibitions, which change regularly. *Closed Sun morn.
Admission charge.*

Imperial War Museum A62
Lambeth Rd SE1. 01-735 8922. National collection on all aspects
of war since 1914, contained in an ex-lunatic asylum. *Closed Sun
morn.*

Madame Tussauds A38
Marylebone Rd NW1. 01-935 6861. Waxen images of the famous
and notorious, life-size and life-like. Chamber of Horrors gets the
adrenalin going. *Admission charge.*

Museum of London A43
London Wall EC2. 01-600 3699. A 3-dimensional biography of the
City and London area. *Closed Sun morn and Mon.*

National Gallery A51
Trafalgar Sq WC2. 01-839 3321. Built 1838 by W. Wilkins and
containing a fine representative collection of the various schools of
painting. *Closed Sun morn.*

Natural History Musuem A57
Cromwell Rd SW7. 01-589 6323. Exhibitions of zoology, entomo-
logy, palaeontology and botany. *Closed Sun morn.*

Planetarium   A38
Marylebone Rd NW1. 01-486 1121. Beginner's guide to the galaxy. The universe is represented hourly on the domed ceiling, with a commentary. *Admission charge.*

Science Museum   A57
Exhibition Rd SW7. 01-589 3456. Large collection of working models and special exhibitions on the history of science and its application to industry. *Closed Sun morn.*

Tate Gallery   B61
Millbank SW1. 01-821 1313. Famous for its representative collections of British paintings from the 16thC to the present day; also rich in foreign paintings and British and European sculpture. *Closed Sun morn.*

Victoria and Albert Museum   A57
Cromwell Rd SW7. 01-589 6371. Vast collection of decorative art from all categories, countries and ages. Over 10 acres of museum! *Closed Sun morn and all Fri.*

Wallace Collection   B38
Hertford House, Manchester Sq W1. 01-935 0687. Fine private collection of paintings furniture, porcelain and armour, bequeathed to the nation by Lady Wallace in 1897. *Closed Sun morn.*

WHEN THE SUN SHINES

Sunny days call for open spaces, water and trees. Try:

Hampstead Heath, NW3
01-340 5603. 790 acres of parkland, sandy hills and wooded valleys. Once haunted by highwaymen, now crowded with visitors to the Bank Holiday fairs and famous inns – The Bull & Bush, Spaniard's and Jack Straw's Castle. Superb views. Also, wander through the streets of Hampstead – famous for its literary and artistic connections, as well as its appealing 'village' atmosphere.

Hyde Park, W1   A47
01-262 5484. 340 acres of Royal parkland with Rotten Row for horse riders, the Serpentine for fishermen, boaters, swimmers and admirers of ducks, and an open-air bar and restaurant for the hungry or thirsty.

Jason's Trip
Opp 60 Blomfield Rd W9. 01-286 4328. Traditional narrow boats make 1½ hour return trips through Regent's Park Zoo to Hampstead Road Locks.

Kensington Gardens, W8   A46
01-937 4848. An elegant addition to Hyde Park, containing Kensington Palace, the peaceful sunken garden, Round Pond, Albert Memorial – and Peter Pan's statue.

Kenwood House
Hampstead La NW3. 01-348 1286. 18thC Robert Adam House,

with fine art collection and superb grounds. On Sat in summer, leading orchestras give lakeside concerts. Take a picnic. Book for tickets on 01-633 1707.

The London Zoo A32
Regent's Pk NW1. 01-722 3333. By Decimus Burton, 1827. Since then, famous architects have designed new quarters for one of the largest animal collections in the world. First class children's zoo. *Admission charge.*

Regent's Park Open Air Theatre B31
Inner Circle, Regent's Pk NW1. 01-486 2431. Round off a fine day by watching a play, usually Shakespearean, in an attractive outdoor setting. *Jun–Aug.*

St James's Park & Green Park, SW1
01-262 5484. The oldest Royal park with a Chinese-style lake, bridge and weeping willows. Richly populated bird sanctuary on Duck Island presided over by the magnificent pelicans.

TAKING TO THE RIVER

Good way to see London when the weather is fine. You can telephone the special River Boat Information Service on 01-730 4812. Below are two of the best trips.

GREENWICH
Westminster Pier B51
Victoria Embankment SW1. 01-930 4097. Boats leave for Greenwich about *every 30 min.*

The 'Cutty Sark
King Willam Wlk SE10. 01-858 3445. Visit one of the great sailing tea clippers. *Closed Sun morn. Admission charge.*

National Maritime Museum
Romney Rd SE10. 01-858 4422. Finest maritime collection in Britain. Incorporates Queen's House by Inigo Jones, 1616, and the Old Royal Observatory with its astronomical instruments and Planetarium. *Closed Mon.*

Royal Naval College
Greenwich SE10. 01-858 2154. Fine group of classical buildings by Webb, Wren and Vanburgh, fronting on to the river. Chapel by James Stuart, Painted Hall by Thornhill. *Closed morns and Thur.*

KEW
Boats leave Westminster Pier for Kew *about every 30 min.*
Royal Botanic Gardens
Kew Rd, Surrey. 01-940 1171. One of the world's great botanic gardens with magnificent Victorian planthouses. 300 acres of green peace and unusual flowers. *Small charge.*

CULTURAL ENTERTAINMENT

For music, opera, ballet or theatre it is wise to book seats in advance at the Box Office (a Ticket Agency will charge commission). If you can face possible disappointment, try for 'returns' just before the performance. Brief details and times appear in *Time Out*, *The London Standard*, and the national newspapers.

MUSIC

Royal Albert Hall   B46
Kensington Gore SW7. 01-589 8212. Huge, Victorian domed hall famous for the 'Proms'. Mainly orchestral and choral, but also pop concerts and meetings.

Royal Festival Hall   A52
South Bank SE1. 01-928 3191. Built 1951 as part of South Bank Arts Centre. Orchestral and choral concerts here, or in adjacent Queen Elizabeth Hall and Purcell Room.

St John's   A61
Smith Sq SW1. 01-222 1061. Solo recitals, chamber, orchestral and choral works in a unique 18thC church. Licensed buffet and art exhibition in the crypt.

Wigmore Hall   B39
36 Wigmore St W1. 01-935 2141. By tradition, visiting musicians make their London debut in its intimate atmosphere. Chiefly chamber music and solo recitals.

OPERA AND BALLET

Coliseum   A51
St Martin's La WC2. 01-836 3161. Opera in English from the English National Opera (and from visiting companies). Also ballet performed for audiences of up to 2,400.

Royal Opera House, Covent Garden   B41
Bow St WC2. 01-240 1066. 24-hr information and bookings 01-240 1911. Where to see the world-famous Royal Opera and Royal Ballet companies. Those in the expensive seats often dress up for the occasion.

Sadler's Wells   B35
Rosebery Av EC1. 01-278 8916. The original well discovered by Thomas Sadler is under a trap-door at the back of the stalls. Birthplace of the Royal Ballet Company; now used by visiting opera and dance companies.

THEATRE

London has had live theatre for seven centuries. Today the greatest concentration of theatres is along, or just off, Shaftesbury Ave, Leicester Sq and within the Covent Garden area. See 'Theatres & Cinemas Map' on page 26.

Barbican (RSC)   A43
Barbican Centre, Barbican EC2. 01-628 8795. Purpose-built for
the Royal Shakespeare Company. A large theatre for large scale
productions and The Pit for the performance work by new British
playwrights. See the Master, revivals and classics.

Criterion   A50
Piccadilly Circus W1. 01-930 3216. A listed building with pre-
served interior. Shows light comedies and straight drama.

Haymarket (Theatre Royal)   A50
Haymarket SW1. 01-930 9832. Originally built in 1720 as 'The
Little Theatre in the Hay'. Present theatre was designed by Nash
in 1821. Stages light plays.

Lyric   B40
Shaftesbury Av W1. 01-437 3686. Oldest theatre in Shaftesbury
Av, built in 1888. Sarah Bernhardt performed here. Today, mainly
plays and musicals.

National Theatre   A52
South Bank SE1. 01-928 2252. The large apron-staged Olivier,
smaller Lyttelton, and adaptable Cottesloe are the home of the
National Theatre Company and stage a wide variety of plays.
Daytime tours take you backstage and into the workshops.

Palladium   B40
8 Argyll St W1. 01-437 7373. Houses top variety shows, the annual
Royal Comman Performance and a pantomime at Christmas.

Vaudeville   A51
Strand WC2. 01-836 9988. Listed building. Originally ran farce
and burlesque, than became straight; which for the most part it
remains.

ROCK, POP AND ALL THAT JAZZ

For live music in a relaxed setting you can't beat the pubs and
clubs. The charge is rarely high and membership, if necessary, is
usually available at the door. For details see *What's On & Where to
Go*, or the music press.

Bull's Head
373 Lonsdale Rd SW13. 01-876 5241. Worth the trip south of the
river to hear good modern jazz, every evening, from top English
and visiting foreign players.

Cock Tavern
360 North End Rd SW6. 01-385 6021. Jazz, disco and an organist
variously on offer in the back bar. *Fri–Sun.*

Greyhound
175 Fulham Palace Rd W6. 01-385 0526. Famous old pub with
interior purpose-built for staging music. Rock, punk and reggae.

Half Moon
93 Lower Richmond Rd, Putney, SW15. 01-788 2387. To the
south again for this large pub with its spacious back room where

live music is played every night and on Sun lunchtime. Jazz, folk, rock, R & B.

Pindar of Wakefield   B34
328 Gray's Inn Rd WC1. 01-837 7269. And now for something completely different — traditional old-time music hall. Join in the choruses if you can. Food in a basket served while you watch. Essential to book.

Rock Garden   B41
6-7 The Piazza, Covent Garden WC2. 01-240 3961. American-style restaurant upstairs and on street level. Downstairs, nightly rock concerts (though never on *Sun*).

Ronnie Scott's   B40
46-49 Frith St W1. 01-439 0747. Enjoy the best jazz in London in a comfortable atmosphere with subtle lighting and good food. *Closed Sun. Admission charge.*

Torrington
4 Lodge La N12. 01-445 4710. Well-known in the pub circuit for some top names in jazz rock. Resident and visiting bands play in the restaurant. *Thur & Sun nights.*

The Venue   A59
160-162 Victoria St SW1. 01-834 5500. Once a cinema, now a disco and rock joint with fast-food. Live bands play from *Mon–Sat to 02.00.* Check the press for details.

STRICTLY FOR THE ENERGETIC

If the mixture of culture and night life is wearing you out, a bit of healthy exercise could work wonders.

SKATING PLACES
These are clubs, but you can join at the door. Pay by the hour and for skate hire. Tuition an optional extra.

Jubilee Hall   B41
Covent Garden Sq WC2. 01-836 2799. Multipurpose sports hall with regular roller skating and roller disco on *Sun afternoons*. Run mainly by cheerful Australians.

Queen's Ice Skating Club   B36
17 Queensway W2. 01-229 0172. If your wheels are running away with you, change to blades and cut a dash on the ice. Crowded and sociable with a licensed bar to help restore lost confidence.

SPORTS CENTRES
If you want to use the more popular facilities it is wise to book in advance.

Crystal Palace National Sports Centre
Crystal Palace SE19. 01-778 0131. Largest multi-sports centre in the country, right in Crystal Palace Park. Facilities include dry-

skiing, skating, squash, swimming. Fully equipped indoor sports hall. *Day membership scheme.*

YMCA: London Central A41
112 Gt Russell St WC1. 01-637 8131. Welcomes local and overseas members of both sexes. Indoor only, including gymnastics, swimming, table tennis and yoga. *Membership necessary.*

WALKING TOURS

A guided walk, usually with a special theme, is an inexpensive way of seeing more of London.

Mysterious Interiors of Hidden London A41
5 Bevan House, Boswell St WC1. 01-405 6191. A morning-long tour of the parts of London that even Londoners don't always reach. Starts from Holborn tube. *Tue–Thur 09.50.*

London Walks
139 Conway Rd, Southgate N14. 01-882 2763. Meet at various tube stations for walks (1½–2hrs) with titles like Legal and Illegal London, An Historic Pub Walk and The Famous Square Mile. *Mar–Nov, Mon–Sun; Nov–Mar, weekends only.*

SINISTER LONDON

The older parts of London are somewhat grisly anyway, with their history of murder, martyrdom and ghosts. But if you relish the gruesome, try these extras.

Discovering London
11 Pennyfield, Worley, Brentwood, Essex. Brentwood 213704. Shuddery organised walks including Evil London, Night Prowl.

Highgate Cemetery
Swains La N6. 01-340 1834. Most graveyards have a certain creepy splendour – this one also has the dust of the famous, including Karl Marx, George Eliot and Faraday.

London Dungeon B54
34 Tooley St SE1. 01-403 0606. A horror museum in suitably unpleasant surroundings – huge damp vaults under London Bridge Station. Scenes of medieval torture garnished with stage blood. *Admission charge.*

Tower of London A55
Tower Hill EC3. 01-709 0765. Grim and famous fortress guarded by Beefeaters and ravens. See Traitors Gate (entrance of the doomed), armoury, executioner's block and axe – and the Crown Jewels. *Admission charge.*

Tower of Ramsgate A55
62 Wapping High St E1. 01-488 2685. At the end of an eerie day, restore the nerves with a drink in this 17thC riverside tavern, where, nearby, Colonel Blood was caught while trying to escape with the Crown Jewels. And below, pirates and smugglers used to be tied to be drowned by the incoming tide.

London is immensely rich in shops, from large department stores to small specialists. The four main West End shopping streets are the very crowded Oxford St for department stores, clothes and shoes; the more sedate Regent St for expensive clothes, china and glass; Tottenham Court Rd for electronics and furniture; and Bond St for luxurious clothes, rugs, jewellery and pictures. *Most shops open 09.00–17.30 Mon–Sat.* Try:

Anything Left Handed   A50
65 Beak St W1. 01-437 3910. For the south-paws back home. More than 100 left-handed gadgets always in stock. *Closed Sat afternoons.*

Covent Garden General Store   B41
111 Long Acre. 01-240 0331. A large and bright store overflowing with gifts and novelties to solve every present problem. Basketware, bags, scarves, cosmetics, stationery and lots of gimmicky gift ideas. *Open to 24.00 Mon–Sat.*

The Design Centre   A50
28 Haymarket SW1. 01-839 8000. And now to raise the tone. Large showroom of the best in British design – all for sale to the descerning.

Fortnum and Mason   A50
181 Piccadilly W1. 01-734 8040. Elegant carpeted store selling luscious selection of unusual bottled and canned foods from all over the world. Worth admiring even if you can't afford to buy.

Foyles   B40
119–125 Charing Cross Rd WC2. 01-437 5660. The biggest of the bookshops. Aims to stock virtually every British book currently in print.

Habitat   A40
196 Tottenham Court Rd W1. 01-631 3880. A member of Terence Conran's hugely successful furniture and household goods chain.

Harrods   B48
Knightsbridge SW1. 01-730 1234. Most famous of British department stores, laden with Royal Warrants. Massive food halls, huge range of clothes, books, animals (stuffed, skinned and living), banking hall, travel and booking agency – in fact, everything.

HMV Record Store   B39
363 Oxford St W1. 01-629 1240. Probably the most comprehensive stock of records and cassettes in London.

Liberty's   B40
Regent St W1. 01-734 1234. Department store especially famous for its printed fabrics. Also particularly good on china, glass and fashion jewellery.

Marks & Spencer   A38 & B40
173 & 458 Oxford St W1. 01-734 4904/935 7954. Two major branches of this British shopping 'institution'. Good quality clothes for adults and children. You can't try things on but an exchange or refund is always forthcoming. Also food, books, etc.

Selfridges B40

400 Oxford St W1. 01-629 1234. Large and hectic department store. Big food hall, huge household department; also clothes, toys, furniture and sports gear. Garage parking.

GOING TO MARKET

Wholesale markets for serious business open around dawn. Small markets or cheap fruit and veg, and 'antique' markets for bargains and rip-offs, usually open shop hours. Here are 3 to look at and 3 to shop in.

Berwick St B40

Soho W1. General market in the heart of Soho; fruit and vegetables are good, prices reasonable. *Closed Sun.*

Billingsgate (wholesale)

North Quay, West India Docks Rd, Isle of Dogs. The new site of London's principal fish market, moved from its age-old location in the city. Still plenty of activity. Can be wet underfoot. *Open from 05.30 Tue–Sat.*

New Covent Garden (wholesale)

Nine Elms SW8. London's foremost wholesale fruit, vegetable and flower market, moved from its Covent Garden site in 1974. *Open from 04.00 Mon–Sat.*

Petticoat Lane B45

Radiates from Middlesex St E1. Huge bustling complex selling everything under the sun; bargains, rubbish and fun. *Sun mornings only.*

Portobello Road

Nr Notting Hill Gate tube W11. Famous flea market. Fruit, veg, flowers, *Mon–Sat.* Antiques, bizarre clothes and a welter of glorious junk, *Sat only.*

Smithfield (wholesale) B43

Charterhouse St EC1. World's largest meat market. Interesting architecture and storage techniques but for most people — 10 acres of horror. *Open from 05.00 Mon–Fri.*

EATING AND DRINKING

FOOD

London can serve English and every kind of foreign food at all prices. This brief selection is just to start you off. Most restaurants open *12.00–15.00, 18.00–22.30.*

Fish and Chips

Almost a national dish in Britain. There are fish and chip shops all over London, of varying quality. Some have tables, most do 'take-

away'; add salt and vinegar to taste and eat them from newspaper in traditional style.

Archduke A52

Concert Hall Approach SE1. 01-928 9370. Appealing wine bar built into a railway arch and abounding with brickwork, red pipes and hanging baskets. Plenty of wines; sausages are a speciality; French à la carte menu too. Live jazz and blues.

Cranks B40

8 Marshall St W1. 01-437 9431. One of the first wholefood vegetarian restaurants. Self-service, light, cheerful, popular. *Closes 20.30 Mon, 20.00 Tue–Sat & all Sun.*

Fawlty Towers B57

516–518 Fulham Rd SW6. 01-736 0240. Zany funhouse, where you can expect the unexpected. Dancing, cabaret and boisterous practical jokes. *Open to 01.00. Closed Sun.*

Flanagan's A38

100 Baker St W1. 01-935 0287. Phoney but enjoyable Victorian dining rooms. Cockney songs, singing waitresses, tripe, jellied eels, fish and chips and syrup pudding. Please don't spit in the sawdust!

Geale's Fish Restaurant

2–4 Farmer St W8. 01-727 7969. Informal restaurant with cheerful service. Good fish and real chips, crab soup, puddings, and wine by the glass. *Closed Sun & Mon.*

Hard Rock Café A49

150 Old Park La W1. 01-629 0382. Excellent hamburger joint with non-stop rock music. Long queues in evening.

Khan's

13 Westbourne Gro W2. 01-727 5420. Vast, bustling Indian restaurant with Oriental arches. Specialities include tandoori bot kebab, kofti dilruba and mutter paneer.

Le Ho Fook B41

15 Gerrard St W1. 01-734 9578. In the heart of Chinatown and much-patronised by Chinese. Excellent cooking, generous portions, but service is slow. Famous for dim sum (steamed savouries in bamboo baskets).

Peppermint Park A51

13-14 Upper St Martin's La WC2. 01-836 5234. Crowded, lively atmosphere in this green and vivid pink restaurant. Cocktail bar and American food.

Tudor Rooms A51

80 St Martin's La WC2. 01-240 3978. Aptly termed a 'medieval theatre restaurant'. Six-course olde English meal served by buxom wenches while troubadours, jesters and a dancing bear entertain. If you don't join in they actually put you in the stocks.

Vasco and Piero's Pavilion Restaurant B40

Academy Cinema, Poland St W1. 01-437 8774. Sample fine Italian cuisine accompanied by guitar music. Seafood salad, stinco arrosto, gâteau soaked in Grand Marnier. *Closed Sun.*

PUBS

The pub is uniquely English and many English pubs are unique. There are historical, literary, sporting and 'theme' pubs and London has more than 7,000. Here are 9 of the best. Usual hours *11.00-15.00, 17.30-23.00 Mon-Sat; 12.00-14.00, 19.00-22.30 Sun. (City pubs close early).*

Cheshire Cheese, Ye Olde
B42

145 Fleet St EC4. 01-353 6170. Rambling old building with low ceilings, oak tables and sawdusted floors above a 14thC crypt. Stout English food – famous for its winter game puddings. *Closes 20.30 and Sat & Sun.*

Cockney Pride
A50

6 Jermyn St SW1. 01-930 5339. Nostalgic reconstruction of a Victorian Cockney pub with traditional pub pianist and sausage and mash for the hungry.

George Inn
B53

77 Borough High St SE1. 01-407 2056. London's only remaining galleried coaching inn. From May to August, Southwark Arts Council puts on Shakespearean plays in the courtyard. Two bars, grill room and restaurant.

Lamb and Flag
A51

33 Rose St WC2. 01-836 4108. 300-year-old pub once known as 'The Bucket of Blood' when bare fist fights were held upstairs. Now a popular, mellow bar. Good lunchtime snacks and a noted real ale. Even more crowded than usual on Burns Night.

Mayflower

117 Rotherhithe St SE16. 01-237 4088. Tudor Inn originally called The Shippe, but renamed when the Mayflower, which set off from nearby, reached America. Licensed to sell English and US postage stamps. Nice restaurant.

Prospect of Whiby

57 Wapping Wall E1. 01-481 1095. Ancient dockland tavern dating back to henry VIII's reign. Once used by so many thieves and smugglers they called it 'The Devils Tavern'. Restaurant with terrace overlooks the river.

St Stephen's Tavern
B51

10 Bridge St SW1. 01-930 3230. The MPs local – a bell rings to call them back to the House to vote. River views from the bar. Upmarket food bar in basement is decorated with political cartoons.

Samuel Pepys
A54

Brooks Wharf, 48 Upper Thames St EC4. 01-248 3691. Converted riverside warehouse. Light airy restaurant and cellar bar with food counter. Transcriptions of Pepys diaries, old lamps and prints. Also ticker-tape news from the wires of UNS and UPI.

Sherlock Holmes
A51

10 Northumberland St WC2. 01-930 2644. Upstairs, next to the restaurant, a reconstruction of the fictitious detective's study. Down in the bar, cuttings, curios and the head of The Hound of the Baskervilles!

Central London **2**

Main Thoroughfares with Bus Routes	
	CHARING CROSS
Main Railway (B.R.) Stations	
Underground Railway Stations	⊖ Embankment
Principal Public Buildings	■ KING'S COLLEGE
Theatres	★ APOLLO
Cinemas	● CLASSIC
Parks and Gardens	

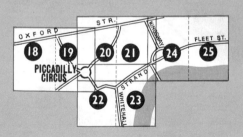

Based upon the Ordnance Survey Maps with the sanction of the Controller of H.M. Stationery Office.

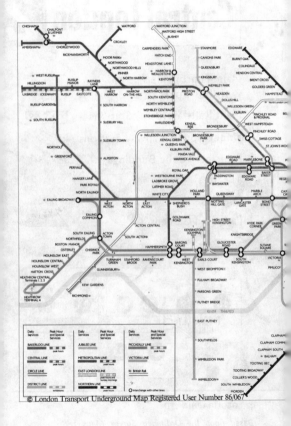

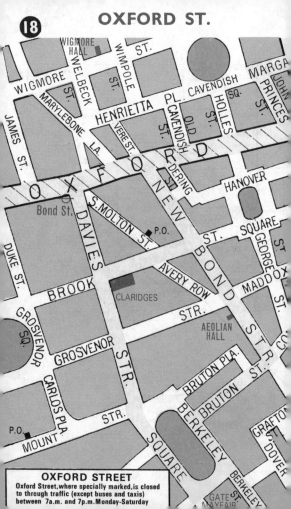

REGENT ST.

19

EROS
CIN.
PICCY
LONDON COVENTRY
PAVILION CINEMA
S. PR. OF
WALES
AUTOMOBILE
ASSOCIATION
ODEON
CINEMA
YORK'S
THEA.
DUKE OF
ST MARTIN'S

EROS
CIRC.
CRITERION
THEA.
Piccadilly Circus
PANTON
ST.

LEICS.
SQ.
IRVING
ST.
LEICESTER SQ.
THEA.

GARRICK
THEA.

LA

P.O

NAT.
PORTRAIT
GALLERY

JERMYN ST.
BEVIS
CENTRE
ODEON
CINEMA

CINECENTA
COMEDY
THEA.
WHITCOMB ST.

NATIONAL
GALLERY

PLAZA
1 & 2
CINEMA

CLASSIC
1, 2 & 3
HAYMARKET
THEA.
(ROYAL) ST.

TRAFALGAR

REGENT STR.
II ST.
P.O.
HER
MAJESTY'S

NELSON'S
COLUMN

Cha

ST. JAMES'S
SQ.

CHARLES
NEW
ZEALAND HO.
PALL MALL E.
CANADA
HO.

SQUARE
Cro

CHARING
CROSS

ST. JAMES'S
SQ.

MALL
COCKSPUR ST.

WATERLOO
PLACE
HO. TER.

ADMIRALTY
ARCH

WHITEHALL
THEA.

W

PALL
GS.
CARLTON
CARLTON
I.C.A.

ROYAL
AUTOMOBILE
CLUB

THE
ADMIRALTY

THE MALL

GUARDS
MEMORIAL

HORSE

GUARDS

PARADE

ST JAMES'S

PARK

DOWNING

GOVERNMENT

COLISEUM THEA.

CHANDOS PL.
AGAR ST.

ADELPHI THEA.

VAUDEVILLE THEA.

SAVOY THEA.

CARTING LA.

WILLIAM IV. ST.

ROYAL SOCIETY OF ARTS

JOHN ADAM ST.

ST. MARTIN IN THE FIELDS

STRAND

VILLIERS ST.

Embankment Gdns.

CLEOPATRA'S NEEDLE

BAND STAND

SOUTH AFRICA HO.

CHARING CROSS ST.

CHARING CROSS

EMBANKMENT

CRAVEN STR.

Embankment

THAMES

NORTHUMBERLAND AV.

HUNGERFORD BRI.

GT. SCOTLAND YD.

WHITEHALL PLA.

PS. TATTERSHALL CASTLE

OLD WAR OFFICE

WHITEHALL CT.

Gardens

VICTORIA

RIVER

HORSEGUARDS AV.

MIN. OF DEFENCE

MIN. OF TECHNOLOGY

WHITEHALL

THE CENOTAPH

LONDON COUNTY HALL

HOLBORN

HOLBORN VIAT.

PATENTS
OFFICE

CITY
TEMPLE

FARRINGDON ST.

"DAILY MIRROR"

RUNIVAL ST.

FETTER LANE

NEW FETTER LANE

SHOE LANE

STONE
CUTTER
ST.

HOLBORN
VIADUCT

RECORD
OFFICE

DR. JOHNSON'S
HO.

GOUGH
SQ.

CHESHIRE
CHEESE

WINE OFFICE
CT.

KING CT.

ST BRIDE ST.

ST BRIDE'S LANE

FLEET   STREET   LUDGTE

LUDGATE
CIRCUS

P.O.

COCK TAVERN

GEOGRAPHIA
LTD.

ST. BRIDE'S
CH.

SALISBURY
SQUARE

BRIDE LA.

NEW BRIDGE ST.

LUDGTE
HILL

PILGRIM
S.

BLACKFRIARS LA.

TEMPLE
CH.

BOURVERIE ST.

DORSET RISE

P.O.

TUDOR   STR.

INNS OF
COURT AND
CHANCERY

THE
TEMPLE

TEMPLE AV.

JOHN CARPENTER ST.

BLACKFRIARS

BANKMENT

H.M.S. PRESIDENT

BLACKFRS BRI.

H.M.S.
RYSANTHEMUM

THAMES

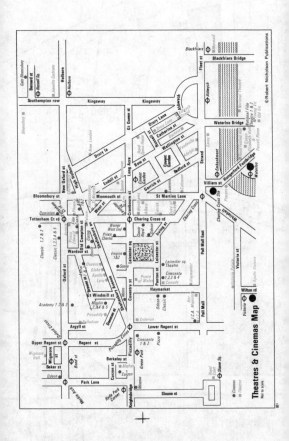

Theatres & Cinemas Map

Not to scale

© Robert Nicholson Publications

London 3

Main Thoroughfares with Bus Routes	
Main Railway (B.R.) Stations	EUSTON
Underground Railway Stations	EMBANKMENT
Principal Public Buildings	NATIONAL GALLERY
Parks and Gardens	
Page Continuation Numbers	32

OXFORD STREET

Oxford Street, where specially marked, is closed to through traffic (except buses and taxis) between 7 a.m. and 7 p.m. Monday-Saturday

---

KEY MAP OVERLEAF ▶

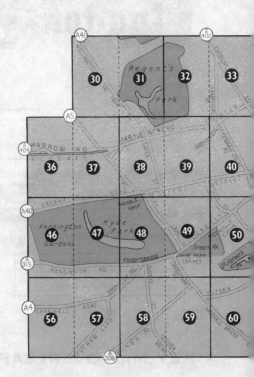

MAPS OF LONDON

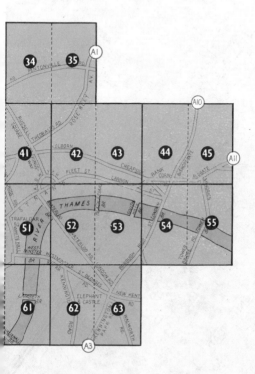

Principal Road Exits
Department of Transport Road Numbers

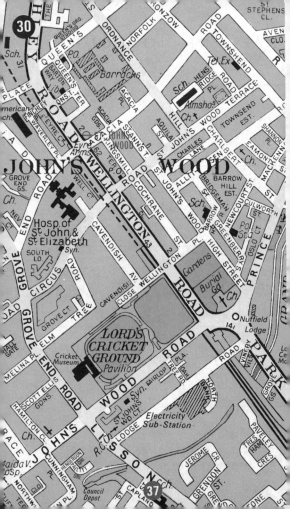

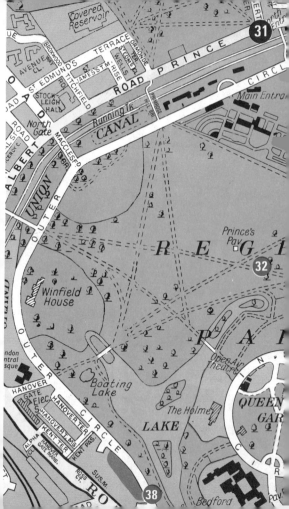

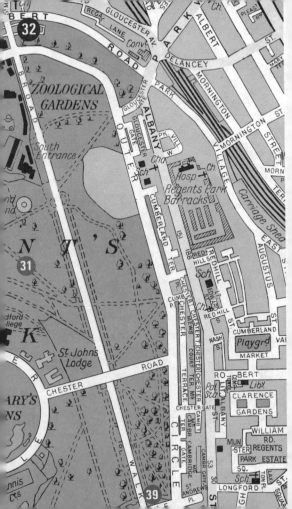

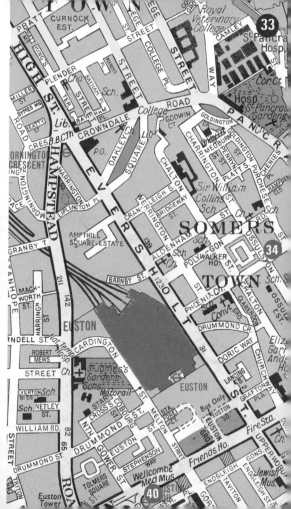

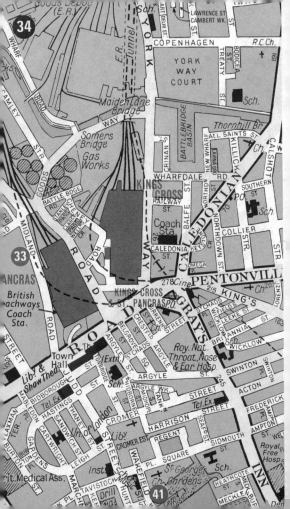

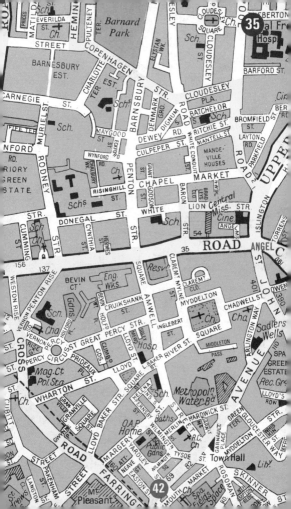

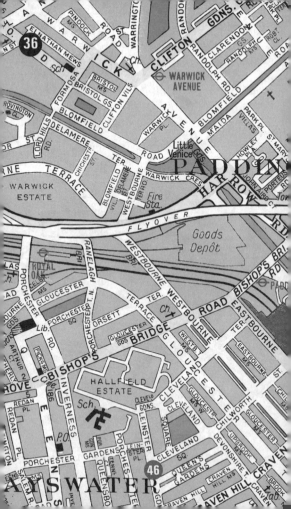

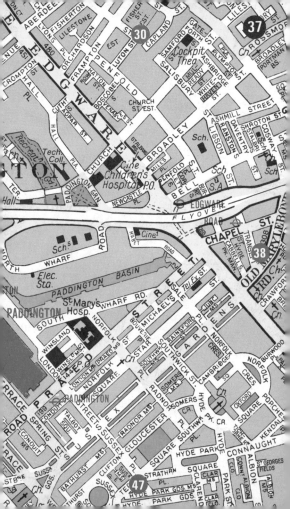

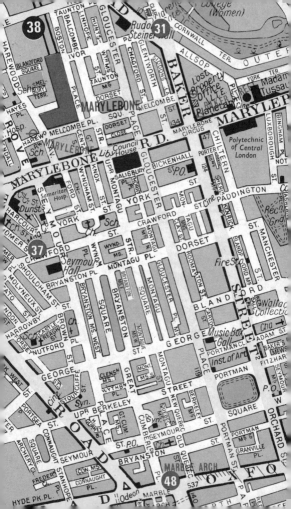

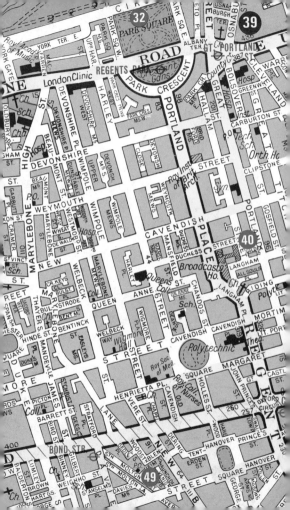

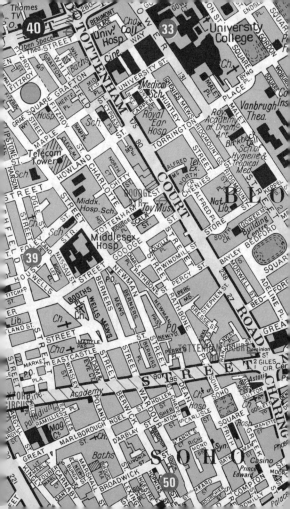

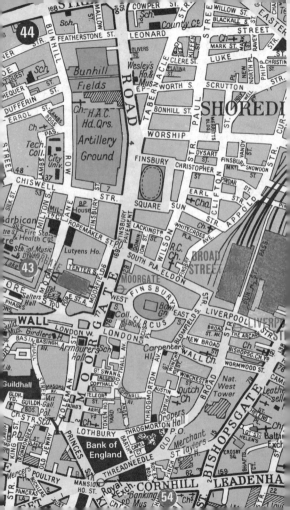

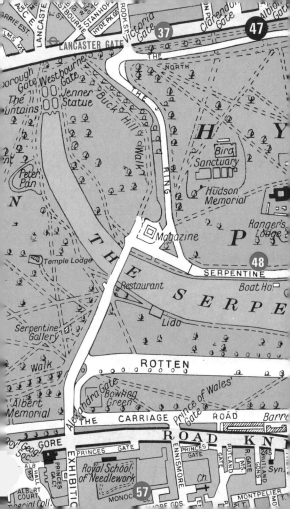

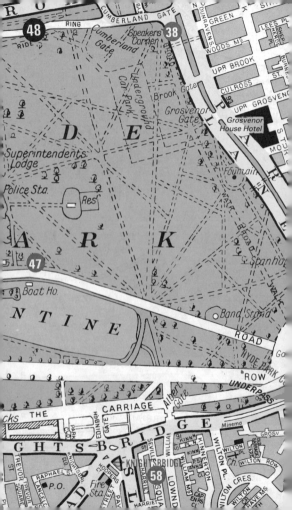

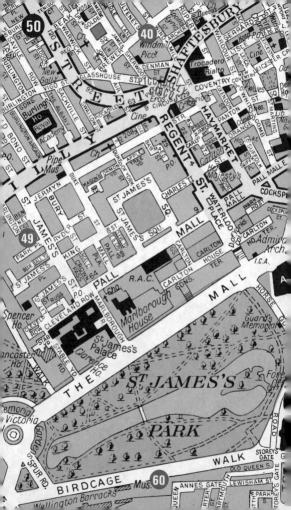

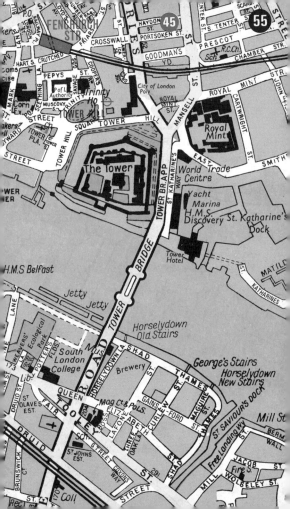

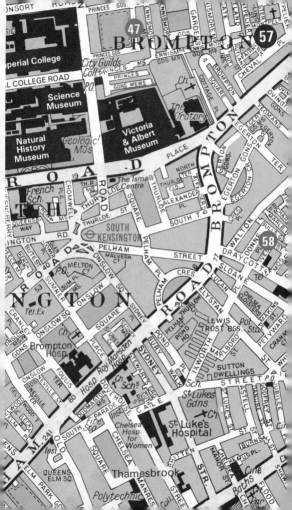

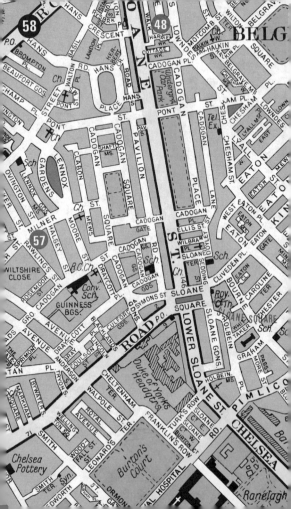

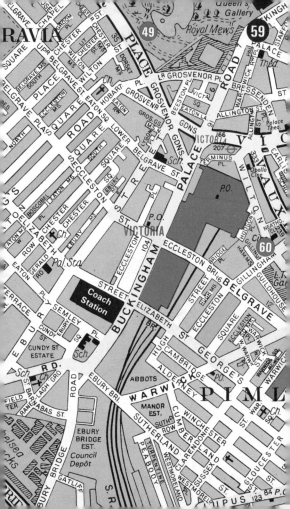

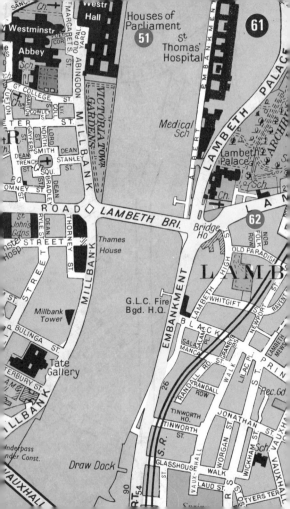

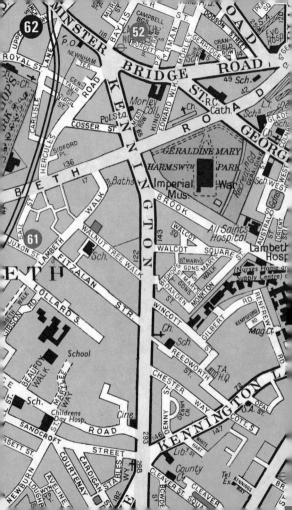

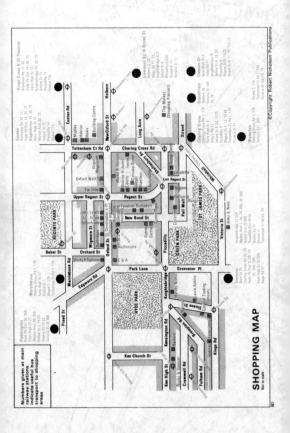

SHOPPING MAP

Not to scale

Numbers given at main railway stations indicate useful bus transport to shopping areas

Paddington
Hyde Pk Cnr 36, 388
Kens High St 27
Marble Arch 7, 15, 36, 388
Oxford St 7, 8, 15, 23
Oxford St 15, 23
Regent St 15, 23
Strand 7, 15, 23
Tottenham Ct Rd 7, 8, 15

Marylebone
Charing Cross 1, 176
Hyde Pk Cnr 74
Kens High St 27
Oxford St 1, 113
Oxford St 2, 13, 30
Strand 1, 176
Tottenham Ct Rd 1, 176

Easton
Euston Rd 10, 18
Hyde Pk Cnr 14, 30, 73
Knightsbridge 14, 30, 73
Kens High St 73
Marble Arch 30, 73
Oxford St 73
Piccadilly 14
Strand 77A

Kings Cross & St Pancras
Brunswick Pk 14, 30
Hyde Pk Cnr 14, 30, 73
Kens High St 73
Piccadilly 14, 18, 73
Piccadilly 14

Liverpool St & Broad St.
Holborn 6, 22
Kens High St 9
Knightsbridge 9, 22
Oxford St 6, 8, 22
Strand 6, 11
Victoria 8, 11

Cannon St.
Kens High St 9
Knightsbridge 9
Oxford St 11
Piccadilly 9
Strand 6, 9, 11, 15, 13/2, 23
Victoria 11

Blackfriars
Kens High St 149
Strand 76, 36

Charing Cross
Hyde Pk Cnr 9
Kens High St 9, 11, 13/15
Oxford St 6, 13, 15/28
Piccadilly 9, 15
Regent St 6, 13/15/29
Strand 6, 9, 11, 15
Victoria 11

Waterloo
Charing Cross 1, 176
Holborn 171, 501

Victoria
Bond St 25
Charing Cross Rd 24, 29
Hyde Pk Cnr 2, 2B, 16
Kens High St 52
Oxford St 2B, 36B, 500
Piccadilly 38
Sloane St 11
Strand 11, 76
Tottenham Ct Rd 24, 29

Euston
Hyde Pk Cnr 30, 73
Hyde Pk Cnr 30, 73
Knightsbridge 14, 30, 73
Kens High St 73
Oxford St 73
Piccadilly 14

Regent St
Liberty
Dickins & Jones
Hamleys
Garrard
Aquascutum

New Bond St
Fenwick
Asprey

Oxford St
D.H. Evans
John Lewis
Selfridges
St. Christopher's Pl
Marks & Spencer

Baker St

Orchard St

Wigmore St

Marylebone Rd

Edgware Rd

Praed St

Park Lane

Piccadilly

Grosvenor Pl

Victoria St

Army & Navy

Pall Mall

Lwr Regent St

Charing Cross Rd

New Oxford St

Tottenham Ct Rd

Holborn

Long Acre

Strand

The Market
(Shopping Precinct)

Maples
Heals
Building Centre

Virgin

Top Shop

Oxford Walk

Upper Regent St

Mothercare

C & A

Knightsbridge

Sloane St

Brompton Rd

Harvey Nichols
Harrods

Laura Ashley
General
Trading Co

Kensington Rd

Ken Church St

Ken High St

Cromwell Rd

Fulham Rd

Kings Rd

Marks & Spencer
Barkers

REGENTS PARK

HYDE PARK

ST JAMES PARK

GREEN PARK

Index 4

ABBREVIATIONS

Arc. — Arcade
Av. — Avenue
Bri. — Bridge
Bldgs. — Buildings
Cir. — Circus
Clo. — Close
Cotts. — Cottages
Ct. — Court
Cres. — Crescent
Dr. — Drive
E. — East
Embk. — Embankment
Est. — Estate

Gdns. — Gardens
Gte. — Gate
Gt. — Great
Gn. — Green
Gro. — Grove
Hl. — Hill
Ho. — House
La. — Lane
Lit. — Little
Lwr. — Lower
Mans. — Mansion
Mkt. — Market
Ms. — Mews

N. — North
Pass. — Passage
Pl. — Place
Rd. — Road
S. — South
Sq. — Square
St. — Street
Ter. — Terrace
Upr. — Upper
Vill. — Villas
Wk. — Walk
W. — West
Yd. — Yard

Note: (1) The letters A or B precede the map page number and indicate whether the street is to be found in the upper half of the page (A), or (B) on the lower half.

(2) Certain streets named in the index are to be found in both the Central London and London map sections. In order to distinguish between the two, the name of the street that is duplicated is given first in a bold type for the Central London section, followed immediately by the same name in ordinary type for the London section.

Abbey Orchard St. SW1	A60	
Abbots La. SE1	B54	
Abbots Manor Est. SW1	B59	
Abchurch La. EC4	A54	
Aberdeen Pl. NW8	B30	
Abingdon St. SW1	A61	
Acacia Gdns. NW8	A30	
Acacia Pl. NW8	A30	
Acacia Rd. NW8	A30	
Achilles Way W1	B49	
Acton St. WC1	B34	
Adam & Eve Ct. W1	B40	
Adam's Row W1	A49	
Adam St.	**21**	
Adam St. W1	B38	
Adam St. WC2	A51	
Addington St. SE1	B52	
Addle Hl. EC4	B43	
Adelaide St.	**23**	
Adelaide St. WC2	A51	
Adeline Pl. WC1	B40	
Adelphi Ter. WC2	A51	
Adpar St. W2	A37	
Agar St.	**21**	
Agar St. WC2	A51	
Air St. W1	B50	
Albany St. NW1	B32	
Albany Ter. NW1	B32	
Albany, The W1	A50	
Albemarle St.	**19**	
Albemarle St. W1	A57	
Alberta Est. SE17	B63	
Alberta St. SE17	B63	
Alderney St. SW1	B59	
Alders Gte. EC1	A43	
Aldford St. W1	A49	
Aldenham St. NW1	A33	
Aldermanbury EC2	B43	
Aldermanbury Sq. EC2	B43	
Aldgate EC3	B44	
Aldgate High St. EC3	B45	
Aldwych	**24**	
Aldwych WC2	B42	
Alexander Pl. SW7	A57	
Alexander Sq. SW3	A57	
Alfred Ms. W1	A40	
Alfred Pl. WC1	A40	
Alie St. E1	B45	
Allhallows La. EC4	B44	
Allington St. SW1	A59	
Allitsen Rd. NW8	A30	
All Saints St. N1	A34	
Allsop Pl. NW1	A38	
All Souls Pl. W1	B39	
Alpha Clo. NW1	B31	
Ambergate St. SE17	B63	
Ambrosden Av. SW1	A60	
Amelia St. SE17	B63	
Amen Ct. EC4	B43	
America Sq. EC3	A55	
America St. SE1	B53	
Ampthill Sq. Est. NW1	A33	
Ampton Pl. WC1	B34	
Ampton St. WC1	B34	
Amwell St. EC1	B35	
Anderson St. SW8	B58	
Angel Ct. EC2	B44	
Angel Ct. SW1	B50	
Angel Ms. N1	A35	
Angel Pl. EC4	B54	
Angel Pl. SE1	A54	
Angel St. EC1	B43	
Ann's Clo. SW1	B48	
Ansdell St. W8	B46	
Ansdell Ter. W8	B46	
Appletree Yd. SW1	A50	
Appold St. EC2	A44	
Aquila St. NW8	A30	
Aquinas St. SE1	B52	
Archer St. W1	A50	
Archery Clo. W2	B38	
Arch St. SE1	A63	
Argent St. SE1	B53	
Argyle St. WC1	B34	
Argyle Wk. WC1	B34	
Argyll St. W1	B40	
Arlington Rd. NW1	A33	
Arlington Sq. N1	A50	
Arlington St. SW1	A50	
Arlington Way EC1	B35	
Arne St. WC2	B41	
Arneway St. SW1	A61	
Arthur Ct. W2	B36	
Arthur St. EC4	A54	
Artillery La. E1	A54	
Artillery Pass. E1	B45	
Artillery Row SW1	A59	
Artizan St. E1	B45	
Arundel St.	**24**	
Arundel St. WC2	A52	
Ashbridge St. NW8	A37	
Ashburn Gdns. SW7	A56	
Ashburn Ms. SW7	A56	
Ashburn Pl. SW7	A56	
Ashland Pl. W1	A38	
Ashmill St. NW1	A37	
Ash Pl. SW1	A59	
Assam St. E1	B45	
Astell St. SW3	B57	
Aster Pl. SE1	B58	
Astwood Ms. SW7	A56	
Atherstone Ms. SW7	B58	
Atterbury St. SW1	B61	
Attneave St. WC1	B35	
Auden Pl. NW1	A30	
Audley St. W1	A58	
Augustus St. NW1	B32	
Austin Friars EC2	B44	
Austral St. SE11	B62	
Aveline St. SE11	B62	
Ave Maria La. EC4	A54	
Avenue Clo. NW8	A31	
Avenue Rd. NW8	A31	
Avenue, The EC3	A54	
Avery Row	**18**	
Avery Row W1	A49	
Avonmouth St. SE1	A63	
Avon Pl. SE1	A63	
Aybrook St. W1	A39	
Aylesbury Rd. SE17	B63	
Aylesbury St. EC1	A43	
Aylesford St. SW1	B60	
Ayres St. SE1	B53	
Babmaes St. SW1	A50	
Back Gravel La. E1	B45	
Back Hl. EC1	A42	
Baden Pl. SE1	A54	
Bainbridge St. WC1	B41	
Bakers Ms. W1	A38	
Baker's Row EC1	A52	

Baker St. NW1	A38	Beak St. W1	A50	Berners Pl. W1	B40
Balcombe St. NW1	A38	Bear Alley EC4	B43	Berners Rd. N1	A35
Balderton St. W1	A38	Bear Gdns. SE1	A53	Berners St. W1	B40
Baldwin's Gdns. EC1	A42	Bear La. SE1	B53	Berryfield Rd. SE17	B63
Balfe St. N1	A34	Bear St. WC2	A50	Berry St. EC1	A43
Balfour Ms. W1	A48	Beatty St. NW1	A50	**Berwick St.**	**19**
Baltic St. EC1	A43	Beauchamp Pl. SW3	A57	Berwick St. W1	B40
Bankend SE1	B53	Beauchamp St. EC1	A42	Bessborough Gdns.	B60
Bankside SE1	A52	Beaufort Gdns. SW3	A58	SW1	
Bankside SE1	B53	Beaufoy Wk. SE11	B62	Bessborough Pl. SW1	B60
Banner St. EC1	A43	Beaumont Ms. W1	A39	Bessborough St. SW1	B60
Barge House Rd. SE1	A52	Beaumont Pl. W1	A40	Bessborough Way	B60
Bark Pl. W2	A46	Beaumont St. W1	A39	SW1	
Barlow Pl. W1	A49	Bedale St. SE1	B54	Bethnal Gn. Rd. E1	A45
Barnby St. NW1	B33	Bedford Av. WC1	B40	Betterton St. WC2	B41
Barnesbury Est. N1	A35	Bedfordbury WC2	A51	Bevin Cl. W1	B35
Barnham St. SE1	B54	Bedford Ct. WC2	A51	Bevin Way WC1	B35
Barnsbury Rd. N1	A35	Bedford Pl. WC1	A41	Bevis Marks EC3	B45
Baron's Pl. SE1	B52	Bedford Row WC1	A42	Bickenhall St. W1	A38
Barrett St. W1	B39	Bedford Sq. WC1	A40	Bidborough St. WC1	B34
Barrie Est. W2	A47	**Bedford St.**	**21**	Billiter St. EC3	A55
Barron Clo. W1	A41	Bedford St. WC2	A51	Bina Gdns. SW5	B56
Barrow Hl. Est. NW8	A30	Bedford Way WC1	A41	Bingham Pl. W1	A38
Barrow Hl. NW8	A30	Beech St. EC2	A43	Binney St. W1	B39
Barter St. WC1	B41	Beeston Pl. SW1	A59	Birchin La. EC3	B44
Bartholomew Clo. EC1	A43	Belgrave Ms. N. SW1	B48	Birdcage Wk. SW1	B50
Bartholomew La. EC2	B44	Belgrave Ms. S. SW1	A59	Bird St. W1	B39
Bartlett St. EC4	B42	Belgrave Ms. W. SW1	A58	Birkenhead St. WC1	B34
Bartletts Pass. EC4	B42	Belgrave Pl. SW1	A59	Bishops Bri. Rd. W2	B36
Barton St. SW1	A61	Belgrave Rd. SW1	B59	Bishops Ct. EC4	B43
Barton Way NW8	A30	Belgrave Sq. SW1	A58	Bishops Ct. WC2	B42
Basil St. SW3	A58	Belgrove St. WC1	B34	Bishopsgate Ch. Yd.	
Basinghall Av. EC2	B43	Bell La. E1	B45	EC2	
Basinghall St. EC2	B43	Bell St. NW1	A37	Bishopsgate EC2	B44
Bastwick St. EC1	A43	Bell Yd. WC2	B42	Bishop's Ter. SE11	B62
Batchelor St. N1	A35	Belvedere Bldgs. SE1	B53	Bittern St. SE1	B53
Bateman St. W1	B40	Belvedere Pl. SE1	A63	Blackburne's Ms. W1	A48
Bath Ter. SE1	A63	Belvedere Rd. SE1	B51	**Blackfriars Bri.**	**25**
Bathurst Ms. W2	B37	Bemerton St. N1	A34	**Blackfriars La.**	**25**
Bathurst St. W2	B37	Bendall Ms. NW1	A38	Blackfriars La. EC4	A53
Battle Bri. La. SE1	B54	Benjamin St. EC1	A43	Blackfriars Pass. EC4	A53
Battle Bri. Rd. NW1	A34	Bennet St. SW1	A50	Blackfriars Rd. SE1	A62
Batt Ms. NW1	A33	Bentinck Ms. W1	B39	Blacklands Ter. SW1	B58
Batt St. NW1	A33	Bentinck St. W1	B39	Black Prince Rd. SE11	B61
Bayham Pl. NW1	A33	Berkeley Ms. W1	B38	Blandford Ms. W1	A38
Bayham St. NW1	A33	**Berkeley Sq.**	**18**	Blandford Sq. NW1	A38
Bayley St. WC1	B40	Berkeley Sq. W1	A49	Blandford St. W1	B38
Baylis Rd. SE1	B52	**Berkeley St.**	**18**	Blenheim St. W1	B39
Bayswater Rd. W2	A46	Bermondsey St. SE1	B54	Blomfield Rd. W9	A36
Beak St.	**19**	Bernard St. WC1	A41	Blomfield St. EC2	B44
		Berners Ms. W1	B40	Blomfield Vill. W2	A36

Bloomburg St. SW1	B60	Brad St. SE1	B52	Broadwick St. W1	B40
Bloomfield Ter. SW1	B58	Braganza St. SE17	B62	Broad Yd. EC1	A42
Bloomsbury Pl. WC1	A41	Braham St. E1	B45	Brockam St. SE1	A63
Bloomsbury Sq. WC1	A41	Braidwood St. SE1	B54	Bromfield St. N1	A35
Bloomsbury St. WC1	B41	Bramham Gdns. SW5	B56	Brompton Pl. SW3	A58
Bloomsbury Way WC1	B41	Brandon St. SE17	A63	Brompton Rd. SW3	B56
Blossom St. E1	A45	Brandon St. SE17	B63	Brompton Sq. SW3	A57
Blue Ball Yd. SW1	B50	Brangton Rd. SE11	B62	Bronti Clo.	B63
Boadicea St. N1	A34	Bray Pl. SW3	B58	Brook Dr. SE11	A62
Boddy's Bri. SE1	A52	Bread St. EC4	B43	Brooke's Ct. EC1	A42
Bolsover St. W1	A39	Breams Bldgs. EC4	B42	Brooke St. EC1	A42
Bolt Ct. EC4	B42	Brechin Pl. SW7	B56	Brook Ms. W2	B36
Bolton Gdns. Ms.		Bremen Rd. SW7	B46	Brook's Ms. W1	A49
SW10	B56	Brendon St. W1	B37	**Brook St.**	**18**
Bolton Gdns. SW5	B56	Bressenden Pl. SW1	A59	Brook St. W1	A49
Boltons, The SW10	B56	**Brewer St.**	**19**	Brook St. W1	B37
Bolton St. W1	A50	Brewer St. W1	A50	Brown Hart Gdns. W1	B38
Bonhill St. EC2	A44	Brew House Yd. EC1	A42	Browning Est. SE17	A63
Booths Pl. W1	B40	Brick St. W1	B49	Browning Ms. W1	A39
Borers St. E1	B45	**Bride La.**	**25**	Browning St. SE17	A63
Borough High St. SE1	A63	Bridewell Pl. EC4	B42	Brownlow Ms. WC1	A42
Borough Rd. SE1	B52	Bridford Ms. W1	A39	Brownlow St. WC1	A42
Boscobel Pl. SW1	A59	Bridgeman St. NW8	A30	Broxwood Way NW8	A31
Boscobel St. NW8	A37	Bridge Pl. SW1	B59	Brune St. E1	B45
Boss St. SE1	B55	Bridge St. SW1	B51	Brunswick Ct. SE1	B55
Boston Pl. NW1	A38	Bridgewater Highwalk		Brunswick Sq. WC1	A41
Boswell Ct. WC1	A41	EC1	A43	Brushfield St. E1	B45
Boswell St. WC1	A41	Bridgewater Sq. EC2	A43	Bruton La. W1	A49
Botolph La. EC3	B44	Bridgewater St. EC2	A43	**Bruton Pl.**	**18**
Boundary Row SE1	B52	Bridgeway St. NW1	A33	Bruton Pl. W1	A49
Bourchier St. W1	B40	Bridle La. W1	A50	**Bruton St.**	**18**
Bourdon Pl. W1	A49	Briset St. EC1	A43	Bruton St. W1	A49
Bourdon St. W1	A49	Bristol Gdns. W9	A36	Bryanston Ms. E. W1	B38
Bourlet Clo. W1	B40	Bristol Ms. W9	A36	Bryanston Ms. W. W1	B38
Bourne Est. EC1	A42	Britannia St. WC1	B34	Bryanston Pl. W1	B38
Bourne St. SW1	B58	Britten St. SW3	B57	Bryanston Sq. W1	B38
Bourne Ter. W2	A36	Britton St. EC1	A43	Bryanston St. W1	B38
Bouverie Pl. W2	B37	Broadbent St. W1	A49	Buckingham Gte. SW1	B59
Bouverie St.	**25**	Broad Ct. WC2	B41	Buckingham Palace Rd. SW1	B59
Bouverie St. EC4	B42	Broadley Portman			
Bowden St. SE11	B62	Bldgs. NW1	A31	Buckingham Pl. SW1	B59
Bow La. EC4	B43	Broadley St. NW8	A37	Buckingham St. WC2	B59
Bowling Gn. La. EC1	A42	Broad Sanctuary SW1	B51	Bucklersbury EC4	B44
Bowling Gn. Pl. SE1	B54	Broad St. Av. EC2	B44	Buckler St. EC4	B44
Bow St.	**21**	Broad St. W1	A49	Buckle St. E1	B45
Bow St. WC2	B41	Broad Wk. NW1	A32	Bucknall St. WC2	B41
Boyfield St. SE1	B53	Broad Wk., The W8	A46	Budge Row EC4	B44
Boyle St. W1	A49	Broad Wk. W1	A48	Bulinga St. SW1	B61
Brackley St. EC1	A43	Broadwall SE1	A52	Bulls Gdns. SW3	A57
Braden St. W9	A36	Broadway SW1	A60	Bulls Head Pl. EC3	B44
Bradleys Clo. N1	A35	**Broadwick St.**	**19**	Bull Wharf La. EC4	A53

Bulst Pl. W1	B39	Cambridge Ter. NW1	B32	Carting La. WC2	A51
Bulstrode St. W1	B39	Camden High St. NW1	A32	Carton St. W1	B38
Bunhill Row EC1	A44	Camden St. NW1	A33	Cartwright Gdns. WC1	B34
Burdett St. SE1	A62	Camlet St. E2	A45	Cartwright St. E1	A55
Burleigh St. WC2	A51	Camley St. NW1	A33	Casson St. E1	B45
Burlington Arc. W1	A50	Camomile St. EC3	B44	Castellain Rd. W9	A36
Burlington Gdns.	**19**	Campbell Bldgs. SE1	A62	Castle La. SW1	A60
Burlington Gdns. W1	A50	Camperdown St. E1	B45	Castlereagh St. W1	B38
Burman St. SE1	A63	Candover St. W1	A40	Castle St. EC1	A42
Burne St. NW1	A37	Canning Ms. W8	A56	Cathedral Pl. EC4	B43
Burnsall St. SW3	B57	Canning Pass. W8	B46	Cathedral St. SE1	B54
Burrell St. SE1	B53	Canning Pl. W8	A56	Catherine Pl. SW1	A60
Burrows Ms. SE1	B52	Cannon Row SW1	B51	**Catherine St.**	**21**
Burton Pl. WC1	B34	Cannon St. EC4	A54	Catherine St. WC2	B41
Burton St. WC1	B34	Canterbury Pl. SE17	B63	Cato St. W1	B38
Burwood Pl. W2	A37	Canvey St. SE1	A53	Catton St. WC1	B41
Bury Ct. EC3	B45	Capel Ct. EC2	B44	Causton St. SW1	B60
Bury St. EC3	B45	Capland St. NW8	A37	Cavaye Pl. SW10	B56
Bury St. SW1	A50	Capper St. WC1	A40	Cavendish Av. NW8	A30
Bury Wk. SW3	B57	Carburton St. W1	A39	Cavendish Clo. NW8	B30
Bush La. EC4	A54	Cardigan Gdns. SW1	F9	Cavendish Pl. W1	B39
Bute St. SW7	B57	Cardigan St. SE11	B62	**Cavendish Sq.**	**18**
Buxton St. E1	A45	Cardington St. NW1	B33	Cavendish Sq. W1	B39
Byng Pl. WC1	B34	**Carey St.**	**24**	Caxton St. SW1	A60
Byward St. EC3	B44	Carey St. WC2	B42	Cecil Ct. WC2	A51
Bywater St. SW3	B58	Carlisle Av. EC3	A55	Celbridge Ms. W2	B36
Cabell St. NW1	A37	Carlisle La. SE1	A62	Centaur St. SE1	A62
Cadogan Gdns. SW1	A58	Carlisle Pl. SW1	A59	Central Mkts. EC1	B43
Cadogan Gte. SW1	A58	Carlisle St. W1	B40	Cerney Ms. W2	B37
Cadogan La. SW1	A58	**Carlos Pl.**	**18**	Chadwell St. EC1	B35
Cadogan Pl. SW1	A58	Carlos Pl. W1	A49	Chadwick St. SW1	A60
Cadogan Sq. SW1	A58	**Carlton Gdns.**	**22**	Chagford St. NW1	A38
Cadogan St. SW3	B58	Carlton Gdns. SW1	B50	Chalbury Wk. N1	A35
Caleb St. SE1	B53	**Carlton House Ter.**	**22**	Chalton St. NW1	A33
Caledonian Rd. N1	B34	Carlton Ho. Ter. SW1	B50	Chambers St. SE16	B55
Caledonia St. N1	A34	Carlton St. SW1	A50	Chamber St. E1	A55
Cale St. SW3	B57	Carlyle Sq. SW3	B57	Chancel St. SE1	B53
Calshot St. N1	A34	Carmelite St. EC4	A52	**Chancery La.**	**24**
Calthorpe St. WC1	A42	**Carnaby St.**	**19**	Chancery La. WC2	B42
Calvin St. E1	A45	Carnaby St. W1	B40	Chance St. E2	A45
Cambert Wk. NW1	A34	Carnegie St. N1	A35	**Chandos Pl.**	**21**
Cambridge Circus	**20**	Caroline Pl. W2	A46	Chandos Pl. WC2	A51
Cambridge Cir. WC2	B40	Caroline Ter. SW1	B58	Chandos St. W1	B39
Cambridge Gte. Ms. NW1	B32	Carpenters Clo. SW1	B48	Chapel Mkt. N1	A35
Cambridge Gte. NW1	B32	Carpenter St. W1	A49	Chapel Pl. W1	B39
Cambridge Pl. W8	B46	Carrington St. W1	B49	Chapel St. NW1	A37
Cambridge Sq. W2	B37	Carter La. EC4	B43	Chapel St. SW1	A59
Cambridge St. SW1	B59	Carter St. SW1	B50	Chapter St. SW1	B60
Cambridge Ter. Ms. NW1	B32	Carthusian St. EC1	A43	**Charing Cross Rd.**	**20**
		Carting La.	**21**	Charing Cross Rd. WC2	B40
				Charing Cross	**22**

Charing Cross WC2	A51	Chester Way SE11	B62	Clements Inn Pass.	B42
Charlbert St. NW8	A30	Cheval Pl. SW7	A57	WC2	
Charles II St.	**22**	Chicheley St. SE1	B51	Clements Inn WC2	B42
Charles II St. SW1	A50	Chichester Rents WC2	B42	Clements La. EC4	B42
Charles La. NW8	A30	Chichester St. SW1	B60	Clennam St. SE1	B53
Charles St. W1	A49	Chichester St. W2	A36	Clenston Ms. W1	B38
Charleston St. SE17	B63	Chicksand Est. E1	A45	Clere Pl. EC2	A44
Charlotte Pl. W1	B40	Chicksand St. E1	B45	Clere St. EC2	A44
Charlotte Rd. EC2	A44	Chiltern St. W1	A38	Clerkenwell Clo. EC1	A42
Charlotte St. W1	A40	Chilton St. E2	A45	Clerkenwell Gn. EC1	A42
Charlotte Ter. N1	A35	Chilworth Ms. W2	B36	Clerkenwell Rd. EC1	A42
Charlwood Pl. SW1	B60	Chilworth St. W2	B36	Cleveland Gdns. W2	B36
Charlwood St. SW1	B60	Chiswell St. EC1	A44	Cleveland Ms. W1	A40
Charrington St. NW1	A33	Chitty St. W1	A40	Cleveland Row SW1	B50
Charterhouse Bldgs.	A43	Christina St. EC2	A44	Cleveland Sq. W2	B36
EC1		Christopher St. EC2	A44	Cleveland St. W1	A39
Charterhouse Ms. EC1	A43	Church St. Est. NW8	A37	Cleveland Ter. W2	B36
Charterhouse Sq. EC1	A43	Church St. W2	A37	**Clifford St.**	**19**
Charterhouse St. EC1	A43	Churchway NW1	A33	Clifford St. W1	A49
Charterhouse St. EC1	A43	Church Yd. Row SE11	B63	Clifton Ct. NW8	B30
Charterhouse St. EC1	A42	Churton Pl. SW1	B60	Clifton Gdns. W9	A36
Cheapside EC2	B43	Churton St. SW1	B60	Clifton Rd. W9	A36
Chelsea Bri. Rd. SW1	A58	Circular Rd. SE1	A63	Clifton St. EC2	A44
Chelsea Cloisters SW3	B57	Circus Pl. EC2	B44	Clifton Ter. W2	B37
Chelsea Manor Gdns.	B57	Circus Rd. NW8	B30	Clifton Vill. W9	A36
SW3		City Rd. EC1	B35	Clink St. SE1	A54
Chelsea Manor St.	B57	City Rd. EC1	A44	Clipstone Ms. W1	A40
SW3		Clabon Ms. SW1	A58	Clipstone St. W1	A39
Chelsea Sq. SW3	B57	Clare Mkt. WC2	B41	Cliveden Pl. SW1	B58
Cheltenham Ter. SW3	B58	Claremont Clo. N1	B35	Cloak La. EC4	A54
Cheney Rd. NW1	A34	Claremont Sq. N1	B35	Clock Pl. SE1	B63
Chenies Pl. NW1	A33	Clarence Gdns. NW1	B32	Cloth Fair EC1	A43
Chenies St. WC1	A40	Clarence Pass. NW1	A34	Cloudesley Pl. N1	A35
Chequer St. EC1	A44	Clarence Ter. NW1	A38	Cloudesley Rd. N1	A35
Chesham Ms. SW1	A58	Clarence Yd. SE17	B63	Cloudesley Sq. N1	A35
Chesham Pl. SW1	A58	Clarendon Clo. W2	B37	Cloudesley St. N1	A35
Chesham St. SW1	A58	Clarendon Gdns. W9	A36	Club Row E2	A45
Cheshire Clo. E2	A45	Clarendon Gro. NW1	B33	Coach & Horses Yd.	A49
Cheshire St. E2	A45	Clarendon Ms. W2	B37	W1	
Chester Clo. SW1	B49	Clarendon Pl. W2	B37	Cobb St. E1	B45
Chester Ct. NW1	B32	Clarendon St. SW1	B59	Coburg St. NW1	B33
Chesterfield Gdns. W1	A49	Clarendon Ter. W9	A36	Cochrane St. NW8	A30
Chesterfield Hl. W1	A49	Clareville Gro. SW7	B56	Cock La. EC1	A43
Chesterfield St. W1	A49	Clareville St. SW7	B56	Cockpit Yd. WC1	A42
Chester Gte. NW1	B32	Clarges Ms. W1	A49	Cockspur Ct. SW1	A50
Chester Ms. SW1	A39	Clarges St. W1	A49	**Cockspur St.**	**22**
Chester Pl. NW1	B32	Claverton St. SW1	B60	Cockspur St. SW1	A50
Chester Rd. NW1	B32	Clay St. W1	A38	Code St. E1	A45
Chester Row SW1	B58	Cleaver Sq. SE11	B62	Coin St. SE1	A52
Chester Sq. SW1	A59	Cleaver St. SE11	B62	Colbeck Ms. SW7	A56
Chester St. SW1	A59	Cleeve Yd. SW1	A50	Colchester St.	B45
Chester Ter. Ms. NW1	B32				
Chester Ter. NW1	B32				

Coldbath St. EC1	A42	
Coleherne Ct. SW5	B56	
Coleman St. EC2	B44	
Cole St. SE1	A63	
Coley St. WC1	A42	
College Gro. NW1	A33	
College Hl. EC4	A54	
College Pl. NW1	A33	
College St. EC4	A54	
College St. NW1	A33	
Collier St. N1	A34	
Collingham Gdns. SW5	B56	
Collingham Pl. SW5	A56	
Collingham Rd. SW5	B56	
Colnbrook St. SE1	A62	
Colombo St. SE1	B52	
Colonnade WC1	A41	
Colville Pl. W1	A40	
Colworth Gro. SE17	B63	
Commercial Rd. E1	B45	
Commercial St. E1	A45	
Compton Clo. NW1	B32	
Compton Pass. EC1	A43	
Compton St. EC1	A43	
Concert Hall App. SE1	B52	
Conduit Ms. W2	B37	
Conduit Pl. W2	B37	
Conduit St.	**18**	
Conduit St. W1	A49	
Connaught Clo. W2	B37	
Connaught Pl. W2	B38	
Connaught Sq. W2	B38	
Connaught St. W2	B37	
Cons St. SE1	B52	
Constitution Hl. SW1	B49	
Content St. SE17	B63	
Conway Ms. W1	A39	
Cooper's La. WC1	A34	
Cooper's Row EC3	A55	
Copenhagen St. N1	A34	
Copenhagen St. N1	A35	
Copperfield St. SE1	B53	
Copthall Av. EC2	B44	
Copthall Clo. EC2	B44	
Coptic St. WC1	B41	
Coral St. SE1	B52	
Coram St. WC1	A41	
Corbet Pl. E1	A45	
Cork St.	**19**	
Cork St. W1	A49	
Corlett St. NW1	A37	
Cornhill EC3	B44	
Cornwall Gdns. SW7	A56	
Cornwall Gdns. Wk. SW7	A56	
Cornwall Ms. S. SW7	A56	
Cornwall Rd. SE1	A52	
Cornwall Ter. NW1	A37	
Corporation Row EC1	A42	
Cosmo Pl. WC1	A41	
Cosser St. SE1	A62	
Cosway St. NW1	B37	
Cotham St. SE17	B63	
Cottage Pl. SW3	A57	
Cottage Wk. SW1	A58	
Cottesmore Gdns. W8	A56	
Cottington St. SE11	B62	
Coulson St. SW3	A50	
Courtenay St. SE11	B62	
Courtfield Gdns. SW5	B56	
Courtfield Ms. SW7	B56	
Courtfield Rd. SW7	B56	
Cousin La. EC4	A54	
Covent Garden	**21**	
Covent Gdn. WC2	A51	
Coventry St.	**20**	
Coventry St. W1	A50	
Cowcross St. EC1	A43	
Cowley St. SW1	A61	
Cowper St. EC2	A44	
Coxons Way SE1	B55	
Cox's Ct. EC1	B43	
Coxson Pl. SE1	B55	
Craig's Ct. SW1	A51	
Cramer St. W1	A38	
Crampton St. SE17	B63	
Cranbourn St.	**20**	
Cranbourn St. WC2 .	A51	
Cranfield Row SE1	A62	
Cranleigh St. NW1	A33	
Cranley Gdns. SW7	B56	
Cranley Ms. SW7	B56	
Cranley Pl. SW7	B57	
Cranmer Ct. SW3	B57	
Craven Hl. Gdns. W2	B36	
Craven Hl. W2	B36	
Craven Hl. Ms. W2	B36	
Craven Pl. WC2	A51	
Craven Rd. W2	B36	
Craven St.	**23**	
Craven St. WC2	A51	
Craven Ter. W2	B36	
Crawford Pass. EC1	A42	
Crawford Pl. W1	B37	
Crawford St. W1	B38	
Crawford St. W1	A38	
Crecent, The EC3	A55	
Creechurch La. EC3	B45	
Creed La. EC4	B43	
Crescent Row EC1	A43	
Cresswell Gdns. SW5	B56	
Cresswell Pl. SW10	B56	
Crestfield St. WC1	B34	
Crinan St. N1	A34	
Cripplegate St. EC1	A43	
Crispin St. E1	B45	
Cromer Est. WC1	B34	
Cromer St. WC1	B34	
Crompton St. W2	A37	
Cromwell Ms. SW7	B57	
Cromwell Pl. SW7	A57	
Crosby Row SE1	B54	
Crosby Sq. EC3	B44	
Cross Keys Clo. W1	B39	
Crosswall EC3	A55	
Crown Ct. WC2	B41	
Crowndale Rd. NW1	A33	
Crown Office Row EC4	A52	
Crown Pass. SW1	B50	
Crucifix La. SE1	B54	
Cruikshank St. WC1	B35	
Crutched Friars EC3	A55	
Cubitt St. WC1	B35	
Culford Gdns. SW1	B58	
Cullum St. EC3	A54	
Culpepper St. N1	A35	
Culross St. W1	A48	
Culworth St. NW8	A30	
Cumberland Gdns. WC1	B35	
Cumberland Gte. W1	B38	
Cumberland Mkt. NW1	B32	
Cumberland Pl. NW1	B32	
Cumberland St. SW1	B59	
Cumberland Ter. NW1	A32	
Cumming St. N1	A35	
Cundy St. Est. SW1	B59	
Cundy St. SW1	B59	
Cunningham Pl. NW8	B30	
Cureton St. SW1	B60	
Curlew St. SE1	B55	
Curnock Est. NW1	A33	
Cursitor St.	**24**	

Cursitor St. EC4	B42
Curtain Rd. EC2	A44
Curzon Pl. W1	B49
Curzon St. W1	B49
Cuthbert St. W2	A37
Cutler St. E1	B45
Cut, The SE1	B52
Cynthia St. N1	A35
Cypress Pl. W1	A40
Dacre St. SW1	A60
Dallington St. EC1	A43
Dane St. WC1	B41
Dante Rd. SE11	B63
Danube St. SW3	B57
Daplyn St. E1	A45
D'arblay St. W1	B40
Dartmouth St. SW1	A60
Daventry St. NW1	A37
Davidge St. SE1	A63
David Ms. W1	A38
Davies Ms. W1	B39
Davies St.	**18**
Davies St. W1	B39
Deacon Way SE17	A63
Dean Bradley St. SW1	A61
Deanery St. W1	A49
Dean Farrar St. SW1	A60
Dean Ryle St. SW1	A61
Deans Ct. EC4	B43
Deans Ms. W1	B39
Dean Stanley St. SW1	A61
Dean St.	**20**
Dean St. W1	B40
Dean's Yd. SW1	A60
Dean Trench St. SW1	A61
Delamere Ter. W2	A36
Delamere St. W2	A36
Delancy St. NW1	A32
Delhi St. N1	A34
Delverton Rd. SE17	B63
Denmark Gro. N1	A35
Denbigh Pl. SW1	B60
Denbigh St. SW1	B60
Denman St. W1	A50
Denmark Pl. WC2	B40
Denmark St.	**20**
Denmark St. WC2	B40
Denning Clo. NW8	B30
Denny Cres. SE11	B62
Denny St. SE11	B62
Denyer St. SW3	B57
Derby Gro. SW1	B51
Derby St. W1	B49
Dering St.	**18**
Dering St. W1	B39
De Vere Gdns. W8	B46
Devonshire Clo. W1	A39
Devonshire Ms. S. W1	A39
Devonshire Ms. W1	A39
Devonshire Ms. W. W1	A39
Devonshire Pl. W1	A39
Devonshire Row EC2	B44
Devonshire Sq. EC2	B45
Devonshire St. W1	A39
Devonshire Ter. W2	B36
De Waldon St. W1	A39
Dewey Rd. N1	A35
Dial Wk., The W8	B46
Diana Pl. NW1	A39
Dickens Sq. SE1	A63
Dignum St. N1	A35
Disney Pl. SE1	B53
Disney St. SE1	B53
Distaff La. EC4	A53
Distin St. SE11	B62
Dock St. E1	A55
Dodson St. SE1	B62
Dolben St. SE1	B53
Dolland St. SE11	B62
Dombey St. WC1	A41
Dominion St. EC2	A44
Donegal St. N1	A35
Donne Pl. SW3	A57
Doon St. SE1	B52
Doric Way NW1	B33
Dorrington St. EC1	A42
Dorset Clo. NW1	A38
Dorset Ms. SW1	A59
Dorset Pl. SW1	B60
Dorset Rise	**25**
Dorset Rd. EC4	B42
Dorset Sq. NW1	A38
Dorset St. W1	A38
Doughty Ms. WC1	A41
Doughty St. WC1	A41
Douglas St. SW1	B60
Douro Pl. W8	B46
Dovehouse St. SW3	B57
Dove Ms. SW5	B56
Dover St.	**18**
Dover St. W1	A49
Dover Yd. W1	A49
Downgate Hl. EC4	A54
Downing St.	**22**
Downing St. SW1	B51
Down St. W1	B49
Doyce St. SE1	B53
Doyley St. SW1	A58
Drake St. WC1	A41
Draycott Av. SW3	A57
Draycott Pl. SW3	B58
Draycott Ter. SW1	B58
Drayton Gdns. SW10	B56
Druid St. SE1	B55
Drummond Cres. NW1	B33
Drummond Gate SW1	B60
Drummond St. NW1	B33
Drum St. E1	B45
Drury La.	**21**
Drury La. WC2	B41
Dryden St. WC2	B41
Duchess Ms. W1	A39
Duchess St. W1	A39
Duchy St. SE1	A52
Duck La. W1	B40
Dudmaston Ms. SW3	B57
Dufferin St. EC1	A44
Dufours Pl. W1	B40
Duke of Wellington Pl. SW1	B49
Duke of York St. SW1	A50
Duke's Ms. W1	B39
Duke's Pl. EC3	B45
Duke's Rd. WC1	B33
Duke St. Hl. SE1	B54
Duke St. SW1	A50
Duke St. W1	B39
Duncannon St. WC2	A51
Duncan St. N1	A35
Dunraven St. W1	A48
Dunstable Ms. W1	A39
Durham Ho. St. WC2	A51
Durham Pl. SW3	B58
Dyott St. WC1	B41
Dysart St. EC2	A44
Eagle Ct. EC1	A43
Eagle Pl. SW1	A50
Eagle St. WC1	B41
Eamont St. NW8	A30
Earlham St.	**20**
Earlham St. WC2	B41
Earl St. EC2	A44
Earnshaw St. WC2	B41

Easleys Ms. W1	B39	Elder St. E1	A45	Euston Sq. NW1	B33
Eastbourne Ms. W2	B36	Eldon Rd. W8	A56	Euston St. NW1	B33
Eastbourne Ter. W2	B36	Eldon St. EC2	B44	Evelyn Gdns. SW7	B56
Eastcastle St. W1	B40	Elephant & Castle SE1	B63	Evelyn Yd. W1	B40
Eastcheap EC3	A54	Elephant Rd. SE17	B63	Everilda St. N1	A35
E. Harding St. EC4	B42	Elizabeth St. SW1	A59	Eversholt St. NW1	A33
Easton St. WC1	B35	Elliot's Row SE11	B63	Everton Bldgs. NW1	B33
E. Poultry Av. EC1	A43	Ellis St. SW1	A58	Ewer St. SE1	B53
E. Smithfield E1	A55	Elm Pk. Gdns. SW7	B57	Exeter St. WC2	A51
East St. EC2	B44	Elm Pk. La. SW3	B56	Exhibition Rd. SW7	B47
East St. SE17	B63	Elm Pl. SW7	B57	Exmouth Mkt. EC1	A42
E. Tenter St. E1	B45	Elms Ms. W2	A47	Exton St. SE1	B52
Eaton Clo. SW1	B58	Elm St. WC1	A42	Eyre Ct. NW8	A30
Eaton Gte. SW1	A58	Elm Tree Clo. NW8	B30	Eyre St. Hl. EC1	A42
Eaton La. SW1	A59	Elm Tree Rd. NW8	B30	Fairbolt St. SW7	A57
Eaton Ms. N. SW1	A58	Elnathan Ms. W9	A36	Fairchild St. EC2	A45
Eaton Ms. S. SW1	A59	Elvaston Ms. SW7	A56	Fairlop Pl. NW8	B30
Eaton Ms. W. SW1	A59	Elvaston Pl. SW7	A56	Fair St. SE1	B55
Eaton Pl. SW1	A58	Elverton St. SW1	A60	Falconberg Ms. W1	B40
Eaton Row SW1	A59	Ely Pl. EC1	B42	Falcon Clo. SE1	B53
Eaton Sq. SW1	A58	Elystan Pl. SW3	B57	Falmouth Rd. SE1	A63
Eaton Ter. SW1	A58	Elystan St. SW3	B57	Fann St. EC1	A43
Eaton Ter. Ms. SW1	A58	Elystan Wk. NW1	A35	Farm St. W1	A49
Ebor St. E1	A45	Embankment Pl. WC2	A51	Farnham Pl. SE1	B53
Ebury Bri. Est. SW1	B59	Emerald St. WC1	A41	Farringdon Rd. EC1	B35
Ebury Bri. Rd. SW1	B59	Emerson Pl. SE1	A53	Farringdon Rd. EC1	A42
Ebury Bri. SW1	B59	Emerson St. SE1	A53	**Farringdon St.**	**25**
Ebury Ms. E. SW1	A59	Emery Hl. St. SW1	A60	Farringdon St. EC1	B42
Ebury Ms. SW1	A59	Emperor's Gte. SW7	A56	Fashion St. E1	B45
Ebury Sq. SW1	B59	**Endell St.**	**21**	Featherstone St. EC1	A44
Ebury St. SW1	B59	Endell St. WC2	B41	Fenchurch Av. EC3	A54
Eccleston Bri. SW1	A59	Endsleigh Gdns. WC1	B33	Fenchurch Bldgs. EC3	B45
Eccleston Ms. SW1	A59	Endsleigh Pl. WC1	A40	Fenchurch Ct. EC3	A54
Eccleston Pl. SW1	B59	Endsleigh St. WC1	B33	Fenchurch St. EC3	A54
Eccleston Sq. Ms. SW1	B59	Enford St. W1	A38	Fenning St. SE1	B54
		English Gdns. SE1	B54	Fernsby St. WC1	B35
Eccleston Sq. SW1	B59	Ennismore Gdns. Ms. SW7	A57	**Fetter La.**	**25**
Eccleston St. SW1	A59			Fetter La. EC4	B42
Eckersley St. E1	A45	Ennismore Gdns. SW7	B47	Field Ct. WC1	A42
Eckford St. N1	A35	Ennismore Ms. SW7	B47	Field Pl. EC1	B35
Edgware Rd. NW8	A37	Ensor Ms. SW7	B56	Fife Ter. N1	A35
Edinburgh Gte. SW1	B48	Epworth St. EC2	A44	Finch La. EC3	B44
Edwards Ms.	B39	Erasmus St. SW1	B60	Finchley Pl. NW8	A30
Egerton Cres. Pl. SW3	A57	Errol St. EC1	A44	Finchley Rd. NW8	A30
Egerton Cres. SW3	A57	Essex Ct. EC4	B42	Finck St. SE1	B52
Egerton Gdns. Ms. SW3	A57	**Essex St.**	**24**	Finsbury Av. EC2	B44
		Essex St. WC2	B42	Finsbury Cir. EC2	B44
Egerton Gdns. SW3	A57	Esterbrooke St. SW1	B60	Finsbury Mkt. EC2	A44
Egerton Pl. SW3	A57	Ethel St. SE17	B63	Finsbury Pavement EC2	A44
Egerton Ter. SW3	A57	Euston Gro. NW1	B33		
Elba Pl. SE17	B63	Euston Rd. NW1	A39	Finsbury Sq. EC2	A44

Finsbury. EC2	A44	
First St. SW3	A57	
Fisher Sq. WC1	B41	
Fisher St. Est. NW8	A37	
Fisherton St. NW8	A37	
Fish St. HI. EC3	A54	
Fitzalan St. SE11	B62	
Fitzhardinge St. W1	B38	
Fitzmaurice Pl. W1	A49	
Fitzroy Ms. W1	A40	
Fitzroy Sq. W1	A40	
Fitzroy St. W1	A40	
Flank St. E1	A55	
Flaxman Ter. WC1	B34	
Fleet La. EC4	B43	
Fleet Sq.	B35	
Fleet St. HI. E1	A45	
Fleet St.	**25**	
Fleet St. WC2	B42	
Fleur De Lis St. E1	A45	
Flitcroft St. WC2	B40	
Flood St. SW3	B57	
Floral St. WC2	A51	
Flower & Dean St. E1	B45	
Foley St. W1	A40	
Folgate St. E1	A45	
Fore Av. EC2	B44	
Fore St. EC2	B44	
Formosa St. W9	A36	
Forset St. W1	B38	
Fort St. E1	B45	
Fortune St. EC1	A43	
Fosbury Ms. W2	A46	
Foster La. EC2	B43	
Foulis Ter. SW7	B57	
Fountain Ct. EC4	A52	
Fourbert's Pl. W1	B40	
Fournier St. E1	A45	
Frampton St. NW8	A37	
Francis St. SW1	A60	
Franklin's Row SW3	B58	
Frazier St. SE1	B52	
Frederick Clo. W2	B38	
Frederick St. WC1	B34	
Friar St. EC4	B43	
Friday St. EC4	A53	
Frith St.	**20**	
Frith St. W1	B40	
Frying Pan All. E1	B45	
Fulham Rd. SW3	B56	
Fulton Ms. W2	A46	
Fulwood Pl. WC1	B42	
Furnival St.	**25**	
Furnival St. EC4	B42	
Fynes St. SW1	A60	
Gage St. WC1	B41	
Gainsford St. SE1	B55	
Galen Pl. WC1	B41	
Gambia St. SE1	B53	
Ganton St. W1	B40	
Garbutt Pl. W1	A39	
Garden Rd. NW8	B30	
Garden Row SE1	B53	
Gardners La. EC4	A53	
Garlick HI. EC4	A53	
Garnault Ms. EC1	B35	
Garnault Pl. EC1	B35	
Garrett St. EC1	A43	
Garrick St. WC2	A51	
Gaspar Ms. SW5	B56	
Gateforth St. NW8	A37	
Gate St. WC2	B41	
Gateways, The SW3	B58	
Gatliff Rd. SW1	B59	
Gaunt St. SE1	B53	
Gayfere St. SW1	A61	
Gaywood St. SE1	A63	
Gees Ct. W1	B39	
Gee St. EC1	A43	
George Inn Yd. SE1	B54	
George Row SE16	B55	
George St. W1	B38	
George Yd. W1	A49	
Gerald Rd. SW1	B59	
Gerrard St. W1	A50	
Gerridge St. SE1	A62	
Ghenies Ms. WC1	A40	
Gibson Rd. SE11	B62	
Gilbert Pl. WC1	B41	
Gilbert Rd. SE11	B62	
Gilbert St. W1	B39	
Gildea St. W1	A39	
Giles Cir. WC1	B40	
Gillingham Ms. SW1	A59	
Gillingham Row SW1	A59	
Gillingham St. SW1	B59	
Gilston Rd. SW10	B56	
Giltspur St. EC1	B43	
Gladstone St. SE1	A62	
Glasgow Ter. SW1	B59	
Glasshill St. SE1	B53	
Glasshouse St.	**19**	
Glasshouse St. W1	A50	
Glasshouse Wk. SE11	B61	
Glasshouse Yd. EC1	A43	
Gledhow Gdns. SW5	B56	
Glendower Pl. SW7	A57	
Glentworth St. NW1	A38	
Globe St. SE1	A63	
Gloucester Av. NW1	A32	
Gloucester Cres. NW1	A32	
Gloucester Gdns. W2	B36	
Gloucester Gte. NW1	A32	
Gloucester Ms. W2	B36	
Gloucester Ms. W. W2	B36	
Gloucester Pl. NW1	A38	
Gloucester Pl. W1	A38	
Gloucester Pl. M. W1	A38	
Gloucester Rd. SW7	A56	
Gloucester Sq. W2	B37	
Gloucester St. SW1	B59	
Gloucester Ter. W2	B36	
Gloucester Way EC1	B35	
Glynde Ms. SW3	A58	
Godfrey St. SW3	B57	
Godliman St. EC4	B43	
Godson St. N1	A35	
Godwin Ct. NW1	A33	
Golden La. EC1	A43	
Golden La. Est. EC1	A43	
Golden Sq.	**19**	
Golden Sq. W1	A50	
Goldford Pl. NW1	A37	
Goldington Cres. NW1	A33	
Goldington St. NW1	A33	
Goldman Clo. E2	A45	
Goodge Pl. W1	A40	
Goodge St. W1	B40	
Goodman St. E1	A55	
Goodman's Yd. E1	A55	
Goods Way NW1	A34	
Goodwins Ct. WC2	A51	
Goose Yd. EC1	B35	
Gordon Sq. WC1	A40	
Gordon St. WC1	B33	
Gore St. SW7	A56	
Goring St. EC3	B45	
Gosfield St. W1	A39	
Goslett Yd. WC2	B40	
Goswell Rd. EC1	B35	
Gough Sq.	**25**	
Gough Sq. EC4	B42	

Name	Ref	Name	Ref	Name	Ref
Gough St. WC1	A42	Gt. Portland St. W1	A39	**Grosvenor Sq.**	**18**
Goulston St. E1	B45	Gt. Pulteney St. W1	B40	Grosvenor Sq. W1	A49
Gower Ct. WC1	A40	**Gt. Queen St.**	**21**	**Grosvenor St.**	**18**
Gower Ms. W1	A40	Gt. Queen St. WC2	B41	Grosvenor St. W1	A49
Gower Pl. WC1	A40	**Gt. Russell St.**	**20**	Grove Ct. NW8	B30
Gower St. WC1	A40	Gt. Russell St. WC1	B40	Grove End Gdns. NW8	A30
Gracechurch St. EC3	A54	Gt. St. Helens EC3	A54	Grove End Rd. NW8	B30
Grafton Ms. W1	A40	Gt. St. Thomas Apostle	A53	Grove Gdns. NW8	B30
Grafton Pl. NW1	B33	EC4		Guildhall Bldgs. EC2	B44
Grafton St.	**18**	**Gt. Scotland Yard**	**23**	Guildhall Yd. EC2	B44
Grafton St. W1	A49	Gt. Scotland Yd. SW1	B51	Guildhouse St. SW1	B59
Grafton Way W1	A40	Gt. Smith St. SW1	A60	Guilford Pl. WC1	A41
Graham Ter. SW3	B58	Gt. Suffolk St. SE1	B53	Guilford St. WC1	A41
Granby La. E1	A45	Gt. Sutton St. EC1	A43	Guinness Bldgs. SE11	B63
Granby St. E2	A45	Gt. Swan Alley EC2	B44	Guinness Bldgs. SW3	B58
Granby Ter. NW1	B33	**Gt. Tichfield St.**	**19**	Gundulf St. SE11	B62
Grand Av. EC1	A43	Gt. Tichfield St. W1	A39	Gunthorpe St. E1	B45
Grange Ct. WC2	B42	Gt. Tower St. EC3	A54	Gutter La. EC2	B43
Grantham Pl. W1	B49	Gt. Turnstile WC2	B42	Guy St. SE1	B54
Grant St. N1	A35	Gt. Winchester St. EC2	B44	Gwynne Pl. WC1	B35
Granville Pl. W1	B38	**Greek St.**	**20**	Habet Rd. W2	A37
Granville Sq. WC1	B35	Greek St. W1	B40	Half Moon Pass E1	B45
Granville St. WC1	B35	Greenberry St. NW8	A30	Half Moon St. W1	A49
Grape St. WC2	B41	Greencoat Pl. SW1	A60	Halkin Arc. SW1	A58
Gravel La. E1	B45	Greencoat Row SW1	A60	Halkin Pl. SW1	A58
Gray's Inn Pl. WC1	A42	Green Dragon Yd. E1	B45	Halkin St. SW1	A58
Gray's Inn Rd. WC1	B34	Greenhills Rents EC1	A43	Hallam St. W1	A39
Gray's Inn Rd. WC1	A42	Green St. W1	A48	Hallfield Est. W2	B36
Gray's Inn Sq. WC1	A42	Green Ter. EC1	B35	Hall Gte. NW8	B30
Gray St. SE1	B52	Greenwell St. W1	A39	Hall Pl. W2	A37
Gt. Castle St. W1	B39	Greet St. SE1	B52	Halsey St. SW3	A58
Gt. Central St. NW1	A38	Grenville Pl. SW7	A56	Hamilton Pl. W1	B49
Gt. Chapel St. W1	B40	Grenville St. WC1	A41	Hamilton Sq. SE1	B54
Gt. College St. SW1	A61	Gresham St. EC2	B43	Hampden Clo. NW1	A33
Gt. Cumberland Ms.	B38	Gresse St. W1	B40	Hampden Gurney Pl.	B38
W1		Greville St. EC1	B42	W1	
Gt. Cumberland Pl. W1	B38	Greycoat Pl. SW1	A60	Hampstead Rd. NW1	A33
Gt. Dover St. SE1	B53	Greycoat St. SW1	A60	Hampton St. SE17	B63
Gt. Eastern St. EC2	A44	Grey Eagle St. E1	A45	Hanbury St. E1	A45
Gt. George St. SW1	B50	Grimsby St. E2	A45	Hand Ct. WC1	B42
Gt. Guildford St. SE1	B53	Grindal St. SE1	B52	Handel St. WC1	A41
Gt. James St. WC1	A41	Groom Pl. SW1	A59	Hankey Pl. SE1	B54
Gt. Marlborough St.	**19**	Grosvenor Cres. SW1	B48	Hanover Gte. NW1	B31
Gt. Marlborough St.	B40	Grosvenor Cres. Ms.	B48	Hanover Gte. Mans.	B31
W1		SW1		NW1	
Gt. Newport St.	**20**	Grosvenor Est. SW1	A60	Hanover Ms. NW1	B31
Gt. Newport St. WC2	A51	Grosvenor Gdns. SW1	A59	**Hanover Sq.**	**18**
Gt. New St. EC4	B42	Grosvenor Gdns. Ms.	A59	Hanover Sq. W1	B39
Gt. Ormond St. WC1	A41	N. SW1		Hanover Ter. NW1	B31
Gt. Percy St. WC1	B35	Grosvenor Hl. W1	A49	Hans Cres. SW1	B48
Gt. Peter St. SW1	A60	Grosvenor Pl. SW1	B49	Hanson St. W1	A40
Gt. Portland St.	**19**				

Hans Pl. SW1	A58	Hays Ms. W1	A49	Holyoake Rd. SE11	B63
Hans Rd. SW3	A58	Haywards Pl. EC1	A43	Holyrood St. SE1	B54
Hans St. SW1	A58	Headfort Pl. SW1	B49	Holywell La. EC2	A45
Hanway Pl. W1	B40	Hearn St. EC2	A45	Holywell Row EC2	A44
Hanway St. W1	B40	Heathcote St. WC1	B34	Homer Row W1	A37
Harcourt St. W1	A38	Heddon St. W1	A50	Homer St. W1	A38
Harcourt Ter. SW10	B56	Helmet Row EC1	A43	Honduras St. EC1	A43
Hardwick St. EC1	B35	Hemingford Rd. N1	A35	Honey La. EC2	B43
Hardwidge St. SE1	B54	Hemus Pl. SW3	B57	Hoopers Ct. SW3	B48
Hare Pl. EC4	B42	Henderson Dr. NW8	B30	Hooper St. E1	A55
Harewood Av. NW1	A38	Heneage La. EC3	B45	Hopetown St. E1	B45
Harewood Pl. W1	B39	Heneage St. E1	B45	Hopkins St. W1	B40
Harewood Row NW1	A38	Henrietta Ms. WC1	B34	Hopton St. SE1	A53
Harley Gdns. SW10	B56	**Henrietta Pl.**	**18**	Horseferry Rd. SW1	A60
Harley Pl. W1	B39	Henrietta Pl. W1	B39	**Horse Guards Av.**	**23**
Harley St. W1	A39	**Henrietta St.**	**21**	Horse Guards Av. SW1	B51
Harp Alley EC4	B42	Henrietta St. WC2	A51	Horse Guards Rd. SW1	B50
Harper Rd. SE1	A63	Hensridge Pl. NW8	A30	Horselydown La. SE1	B55
Harp La. EC3	A54	Herbal Hl. EC1	A42	Hosier La. EC1	B42
Harpur St. WC1	A41	Herbert Cres. SW1	A58	Houghton St. WC2	B41
Harriet St. SW1	B48	Herbrand St. WC1	B34	Houndsditch EC3	B44
Harriet Wk. SW1	B48	Hercules Rd. SE1	A62	Howick Pl. SW1	A60
Harrington Gdns. SW7	B56	Hereford Sq. SW7	B56	Howland Ms. E. W1	A40
Harrington Rd. SW7	A56	Hermes St. N1	A35	Howland Ms. W. W1	A40
Harrington Sq. NW1	A33	Herrick St. SW1	B60	Howland St. W1	A40
Harrington St. NW1	B33	Hertford Pl. W1	A40	Howley Pl. W2	A36
Harrison St. WC1	B34	Hertford St. W1	B49	Hudson Pl. SW1	A59
Harrowby St. W1	B38	Hesper Ms. SW5	B56	Huggin Hl. EC4	A53
Harrow Pl. E1	B45	Heygate St. SE17	B63	Hugh Ms. SW1	B59
Hart St. EC3	A55	Hide Pl. SW1	B60	Hugh St. SW1	B59
Hasker St. SW3	A58	**High Holborn**	**21**	**Hungerford Bri.**	**23**
Hastings St. WC1	B34	High Holborn WC1	B41	Hunter St. WC1	B34
Hatfield St. SE1	A52	High Timber St. EC4	A53	Huntley St. WC1	A40
Hatherley Gro. W2	B36	Hills Pl. W1	B40	Hunton St. E1	A45
Hatherley St. SW1	B60	**Hill St.**	**18**	Huntsworth Ms. NW1	A38
Hatton Gdn. EC1	A42	Hill St. W1	A49	Hyde Park Corner W1	B49
Hatton Pl. EC1	A42	**Hind Ct.**	**25**	Hyde Pk. Cres. W2	B37
Hatton Row NW8	A37	Hind Ct. EC4	B42	Hyde Pk. Gdns. W2	A47
Hatton St. NW8	A37	Hinde St. W1	B39	Hyde Pk. Gdns. W2	B37
Hatton Wall EC1	A42	Hobart Pl. SW1	A59	Hyde Pk. Gdns. Ms. W2	B37
Haunch Of Venison Yd. W1	B39	Holbein Ms. SW3	B58	
Havelock St. N1	A34	Holbein Pl. SW1	B58	Hyde Pk. Gte. SW7	B46
Haydon St. EC3	A55	**Holborn WC1**	B42	Hyde Pk. Gte. Ms. SW7	B46
Hayes Pl. NW1	A38	Holborn Cir. EC1	B42	
Hay Hl. W1	A49	**Holborn Viaduct**	**25**	Hyde Pk. Mans. NW1	A37
Hayles St. SE11	B63	Holborn Viaduct EC1	B42	Hyde Pk. Pl. W2	B38
Haymarket	**22**	Holford Pl. WC1	B35	Hyde Pk. Sq. W2	B37
Haymarket SW1	A50	Holland St. SE1	A53	Hyde Pk. St. W2	B37
Hayne St. EC1	A43	Hollen St. W1	B40	Idol La. EC3	A54
Hays La. SE1	B54	**Holles St.**	**18**	Iliffe St. SE17	B63
		Holles St. W1	B39	Iliffe Yd. SE17	B63

Imperial Institute Rd. SW7	A56	Juxon St. SE11	A62	King's Ms. WC1	A42
India St. EC3	A55	Kean St. WC2	B41	Kingsmill Ter. NW8	A30
Ingestre Pl. W1	B40	Keeley St. WC2	B41	Kings Pl. SE1	A63
Inglebert St. EC1	B35	Kelso Pl. W8	A56	King's Rd. SW1	A58
Inner Circle NW1	B31	Kemble St.	21	King's Scholar's Pass. SW1	A60
Insurance St. WC1	B35	Kemble St. WC2	B41		
Inverness Ms. W2	B36	Kempsford Rd. SE11	B62	King's Ter. NW1	A33
Inverness Pl. W2	A46	Kendall Pl. W1	B38	King St.	21
Inverness Ter. W2	B36	Kendal St. W2	B37	King St. EC2	B44
Ireland Yd. EC4	B43	Kendrick Ms. SW7	A57	King St. SW1	B50
Ironmonger La. EC2	B44	Kennings Way SE11	B62	King St. WC2	A51
Irving St.	20	Kennington La. SE11	B62	Kingsway	21
Irving St. WC2	A50	Kennington Rd. SE1	A62	Kingsway WC2	B41
Isabella St. SE1	B52	Kenrick Pl. W1	A38	King William St. EC4	B44
Islington High St. N1	A35	Kensington Ct. W8	A46	Kinnerton Pl. N. SW1	B48
Ives St. SW3	B57	Kensington Ct. Pl. W8	A46	Kinnerton Pl. S. SW1	B48
Ixworth Pl. SW3	B57	Kensington Gdns. Sq. W2	B36	Kinnerton St. SW1	B48
Jacobs Well Pl. W1	B39	Kensington Gte. W8	A56	Kipling Est. SE1	B54
James St.	21	Kensington Gore SW7	A46	Kipling St. SE1	B54
James St. W1	B39	Kensington Pal. Gdns. W8	A46	Kirby Gro. SE1	B54
James St. WC2	B41			Kirby St. EC1	A42
Jay Ms. SW7	B46	Kensington Rd. W8	A46	Knightrider St. EC4	A53
Jermyn St.	19	Kensington Sq. W8	A46	Knightsbridge SW7	B47
Jermyn St. SW1	A50	Kenton St. WC1	B34	Knightsbridge Clo. SW1	B48
Jerome Cres. NW8	B30	Kent Pass NW1	B31		
Jerome St. E1	A45	Kent Ter. NW1	B31	Knox St. W1	A38
Jerusalem Pass. EC1	A43	Keppel Row SE1	B53	Kynance Ms. SW7	A56
Jewry St. EC3	B45	Keppel St. WC1	A40	Kynance Pl. SW7	A56
Joan St. SE1	B52	Ker St. E2	A45	Lackington St. EC2	A44
Jockey's Flds. WC1	A42	Keystone Cres. N1	A34	Lafone St. SE1	B55
Johanna St. SE1	B52	Keyworth St. SE1	B53	Lambeth High St. SE1	B61
John Adam St.	23	Kiffen St. EC2	A44	Lambeth Ms. SE11	B61
John Adam St. WC2	A51	Killick St. N1	A34	Lambeth Palace Rd. SE1	A61
John Aird Ct.	A36	King & Queen St. SE17	B63		
John Carpenter St.	25			Lambeth Rd. SE1	A61
John Carpenter St. EC4	A52	King Charles St. SW1	B51	Lambeth St. E1	B45
John Felton Rd. SE16	B55	King Edward St. EC1	B43	Lambeth Wk. SE11	B61
John Fisher St. E1	A55	King Edward Wk. SE1	A62	Lambs Bldgs. EC1	A44
John Islip St. SW1	B60	King James St. SE1	A63	Lambs Conduit Pass. WC1	A41
John Prince's St.	18	King John Ct. EC2	A45		
John Prince's St. W1	B39	Kingly Ct. W1	A50	Lambs Conduit St. WC1	A41
John's Ms. WC1	A42	Kingly St.	19	Lambs Pass. EC1	A44
Johnsons Pl. SW1	B60	Kingly St. W1	B40	Lamb St. E1	A45
John St. WC1	A42	Kings Arms Yd. EC2	B44	Lamlash St. SE11	A63
Joiner St. SE1	B54	King's Bench St. SE1	B53	Lanark Pl. W9	A36
Jonathan St. SE11	B61	King's Bench Wk. EC4	A52	Lancaster Ct. W2	A46
Jones St. W1	A49	Kingscote St. EC4	A53	Lancaster Gte. W2	A46
Jubilee Pl. SW3	B57	King's Cross Rd. WC1	B34	Lancaster Ms. W2	B36
Judd St. WC1	B34	King's Hd. Yd. SE1	B54	Lancaster Pl.	23
Junction Ms. W2	B37	Kingsley Ms. W8	A56	Lancaster Pl. WC2	A51

Lancaster St. SE1	A53
Lancaster Ter. W2	A47
Lancelot Pl. SW7	B48
Lancing St. NW1	B33
Landon Pl. SW1	A58
Lanfranc St. SE1	A62
Langdon Pl. SW1	A58
Langford Ct. NW8	A30
Langford Pl. NW8	A30
Langham Pl. W1	B39
Langham St. W1	B39
Langley St. WC2	B41
Langton Cl. WC1	B35
Lansdowne Row W1	A49
Lansdowne Ter. WC1	A41
Lant St. SE1	B53
Larcom St. SE17	B63
Laud St. SE11	B61
Launcelot St. SE1	B52
Launceston Pl. W8	A56
Laverton Pl. SW5	B56
Lavina Gro. N1	A34
Lavington St. SE1	B53
Lawrence La. EC2	B43
Lawrence Pountney Hl. EC4	A54
Lawrence Pountney La. EC4	A54
Lawrence St. NW1	A34
Laxton Pl. NW1	B32
Laystall St. EC1	A42
Layton Rd. N1	A35
Leadenhall Pl. EC3	B44
Leadenhall St. EC3	B44
Leake Ct. SE1	B52
Leake St. SE1	B52
Leather La. EC1	A42
Leathermarket St. SE1	B54
Lecky St. SW7	B57
Leeke St. WC1	B34
Lees Pl. W1	A48
Leicester Ct. WC2	A50
Leicester Sq	**20**
Leicester Sq. WC2	A50
Leicester St. WC2	A50
Leigh Hunt St. SE1	B53
Leigh St. WC1	B34
Leinster Gdns. W2	A36
Leinster M. W2	A46
Leinster Pl. W2	B36
Leinster Ter. W2	A46
Leman St. E2	B45
Lennox Gdns. SW1	A58
Lennox Gdns. Ms. SW1	A58
Lenthall Pl. SW7	A56
Leonard's Ter. SW3	B57
Leonard St. EC2	A44
Leo Yd. EC1	A43
Leveret St. SW3	B57
Lewisham St. SW1	B50
Lewis Trust Bldgs. SW3	B57
Lexham Gdns. W8	A56
Lexham Wk. W8	A56
Lexington St.	**19**
Lexington St. W1	B40
Leyden St. E1	B45
Library St. SE1	A63
Ligonier St. E2	A45
Lilac Pl. SE11	B61
Lilestone Est. NW8	A37
Lilestone St. NW8	A37
Lillington Gdns. Est. SW1	B60
Lime St. EC3	A54
Lincoln's Inn Fields	**24**
Lincoln's Inn Flds. WC2	B44
Lincoln St. SW3	B58
Lindsey St. EC1	A43
Linhope St. NW1	A38
Liplington Pl. NW1	A33
Lisle St.	**20**
Lisle St. WC2	A50
Lisson Gro. NW8	B30
Lisson St. NW1	A37
Litchfield St. WC2	B41
Lit. Albany St. NW1	B32
Lit. Argyll St. W1	B40
Lit. Boltons, The SW10	B56
Lit. Britain EC1	B43
Lit. Chester St. SW1	A59
Lit. College St. SW1	A61
Lit. Dorrit Ct. SE1	B53
Lit. Edward St. NW1	B32
Lit. George St. SW1	B51
Lit. Marlborough St. W1	B40
Lit. Newport St. WC2	A50
Lit. New St. EC4	B42
Lit. Portland St. N1	B39
Lit. Russell St. WC1	B41
Lit. St. James's St. SW1	B50
Lit. Smith St. SW1	A60
Lit. Somerset St. E1	B45
Lit. Tichfield St. W1	B39
Lit. Trinity La. EC4	A54
Lit. Turnstile St. WC2	B41
Liverpool Rd. N1	A35
Liverpool St. EC2	B44
Livonia St. W1	B40
Lloyd Baker St. WC1	B35
Lloyds Av. EC3	B44
Lloyd Sq. WC1	B35
Lloyd's Row EC1	B35
Lloyd St. WC1	B35
Lockyer St. SE1	B54
Lodge Rd. NW8	B30
Lolesworth Clo.	B45
Lolesworth St. E1	B45
Lollard Pl. SE11	B62
Lollard St. SE11	B62
Loman St. SE1	B53
Lombard La. EC4	B42
Lombard St. EC3	B44
London Bridge St. SE1	B54
London Ms. W2	B37
London Rd. SE1	A63
London St. EC3	A55
London St. W2	B37
London Wall EC2	B43
Long Acre	**21**
Long Acre WC2	A51
Longford St. NW1	B32
Long La. EC1	A43
Long La. SE1	B54
Longmoor Ct. NW1	B60
Longville Rd. SE11	B63
Long Yd. WC1	A41
Lord Hills Rd. W2	A36
Lord North St. SW1	A61
Lorenzo St. WC1	B34
Lothbury EC2	B44
Loudoun Rd. NW8	A30
Loughborough St. SE11	B62
Lovat La. EC3	A54
Love La. EC2	B43
Lwr. Belgrave St. SW1	A59
Lwr. Grosvenor Pl. SW1	A59
Lwr. James St. W1	A50

Lwr. John St. W1 A50
Lwr. Marsh SE1 B52
Lwr. Newport St. WC2 A50
Lwr. Sloane St. SW1 B58
Lwr. Thames St. EC3 A54
Lowndes Clo. SW1 A58
Lowndes Pl. SW1 A58
Lowndes Sq. SW1 B48
Lowndes St. SW1 A58
Loxham St. WC1 B34
Lucan Pl. SW3 B57
Ludgate Circus **25**
Ludgate Cir. EC4 B43
Ludgate Hill **25**
Ludgate Hl. EC4 B43
Ludgate Sq. EC4 B43
Luke St. EC2 A44
Lumley St. W1 B39
Lupus St. SW1 B59
Luton St. NW8 A37
Luxborough St. W1 A38
Lyall Ms. E. SW1 A58
Lyall Ms. W. SW1 A58
Lyall St. SW1 A58
Lygon Pl. SW1 A59
Lyons Pl. NW8 A37
Mabledon Pl. WC1 B34
Macclesfield Bri. NW8 A31
Macclesfield St. W1 A50
Macfarren Pl. NW1 A39
Mackennal St. NW8 A30
Macklin St. WC2 B41
Mackworth St. NW1 B33
Maddox St. **18**
Maddox St. W1 A49
Magdalen St. SE1 B54
Magpie All. EC4 B42
Maguire St. SE1 B55
Maida Av. W2 A36
Maiden La. **21**
Maiden La. WC2 A51
Maidstone Bldgs. SE1 B53
Makins St. SW3 B57
Malet Pl. WC1 A40
Malet St. WC1 A40
Mallory St. NW8 A37
Mallow St. EC1 A44
Mall, The **22**
Mall, The SW1 B50
Maltravers St. WC2 A52
Malvern Ct. SW7 A57

Manchester Sq. W1 B38
Manchester St. W1 A38
Mandeville Hos. N1 A35
Mandeville Pl. W1 B39
Manette St. W1 B40
Manningtree St. E1 B45
Manor Pl. SE17 B63
Manresa Rd. SW3 B57
Mansell St. E1 B45
Mansfield Ms. W1 A39
Mansfield St. W1 A39
Mansion Ho. St. EC2 B44
Manson Ms. SW7 B56
Manson Pl. SW7 B56
Mantell St. N1 A40
Maple Pl. W1 A40
Maple St. W1 A40
Macquire St. SE1 B55
Marble Arch W1 B38
Marchmont St. WC1 B34
Margaret St. **18**
Margaret St. W1 B39
Margery St. WC1 B35
Market Ms. W1 B49
Market Pl. W1 B40
Markham Sq. SW3 A55
Markham St. SW3 B57
Mark La. EC3 A55
Mark St. EC2 A44
Marlborough All. SE1 A52
Marlborough Bldgs. SW3
Marlborough Clo. SE17 B63
Marlborough Ct. W1 B40
Marlborough Hl. NW8 A30
Marlborough Rd. SW1 B50
Marlborough St. SW3 B57
Marloes, The NW8 A30
Marshall Gdns. SE1 A63
Marshall St. W1 B40
Marshalsea Rd. SE1 B53
Marsham St. SW1 A60
Martin La. EC4 A54
Martlett Ct. WC2 B41
Mart St. WC2 B41
Marylebone Cir. NW1 A38
Marylebone High St. W1 B39
Marylebone La. **18**
Marylebone La. W1 B39

Marylebone Ms. W1 B39
Marylebone Pass. W1 B40
Marylebone Rd. NW1 A38
Marylebone St. W1 A39
Marylee Way SE11 B62
Mary Ter. NW1 A32
Mason's Arms Ms. W1 B39
Masons Av. EC2 B44
Mason St. SW1 A50
Matilda St. N1 A35
Mathew Parker St. SW1 A60
Maunsel St. SW1 A60
Mayfair Pl. W1 A49
Maygood St. N1 A35
Mays Ct. WC2 A51
Mcleods Ms. SW7 A56
Meadow Row SE1 A62
Meadow Row SE1 A63
Meard St. W1 B40
Mecklenburgh Pl. WC1 A41
Mecklenburgh Sq. WC1 B34
Medburn St. NW1 A33
Medcalf Pl. EC1 B35
Medway St. SW1 A60
Melbourne Pl. WC2 B42
Melbury Ter. NW1 A38
Melcombe Pl. NW1 A38
Melcombe St. NW1 A38
Melior St. SE1 B54
Melton Ct. SW7 B57
Melton St. NW1 B33
Mepham St. SE1 B52
Mercer St. WC2 B41
Meredith St. EC1 B35
Merlin St. WC1 B35
Mermaid Ct. SE1 B54
Merrick Sq. SE1 A63
Merritts Bldgs. EC2 A44
Meymott St. SE1 B52
Middlesex St. E1 B45
Middle St. EC1 A43
Middle Temple La. **24**
Middle Temple La. EC4 B42
Middleton Pass. EC1 B35
Midford Pl. W1 A40
Midhope St. WC1 B34
Midland Rd. NW1 A34
Milborne Gro. SW10 B56
Milcote St. SE1 A63
Miles La. EC4 A54

Miles Pl. NW1	A37	Moor La. EC2	A44	New Bridge St.	25
Milford La. WC2	A52	Moor La. EC2	B44	New Bridge St. EC4	B43
Milk St. EC2	B43	Moor St. W1	B40	New Broad St. EC2	B44
Millbank SW1	A61	Morecambe St. SE17	B63	Newburgh St. W1	B40
Miller St. NW1	A33	Moreton Pl. SW1	B60	New Burlington Pl. W1	A50
Millmans St. WC1	A41	Moreton St. SW1	B60	New Burlington St.	19
Mill St. SE1	B55	Moreton Ter. SW1	B60	New Burlington St. W1	A50
Mill St. W1	B39	Morgan's La. SE1	B54	Newburn St. SE11	B62
Milner St. SW3	A58	Morley St. SE1	A62	Newbury St. EC1	A43
Milroy Wk. SE1	A52	Mornington Cres. NW1	A33	Newcastle Ct. EC4	A54
Milton Ct. EC2	A44	Mornington Pl. NW1	A32	Newcastle Pl. W2	A37
Milton St. EC2	A44	Mornington St. NW1	A32	New Cavendish St. W1	B39
Mincing La. EC3	A54	Mornington Ter. NW1	A32	New Change EC4	B43
Minera Ms. SW1	A58	Morocco St. SE1	B54	Newcomen St. SE1	B54
Minories EC3	B45	Morpeth Ter. SW1	A60	New Compton St.	20
Mint St. SE1	B53	Mortimer Mkt. WC1	A40	New Compton St. WC2	B41
Mitchell St. EC1	A43	Mortimer St. W1	B39	New Ct. WC2	B42
Mitre Ct. EC2	B43	Morton Pl. SE1	A62	Newcourt St. NW8	A30
Mitre Rd. SE1	B52	Morwell St. WC1	B40	New Coventry St. W1	A50
Mitre St. EC3	B45	Moscow Pl. W2	B36	New Fetter La. EC4	B43
Model Bldgs. WC1	B35	Mossop St. SW3	B57	Newgate St. EC1	B43
Molyneux St. W1	B38	Motcomb St. SW1	A58	New Goulston St. E1	B45
Monck St. SW1	A60	Mount Pleasant WC1	A42	Newington Butts SE11	B63
Monkton St. SE11	B62	Mount Row W1	A49	Newington Causeway	A63
Monkwell Sq. EC2	B43	Mount St.	18	SE1	
Monmouth St.	20	Mount St. W1	A48	New Inn St. EC2	A45
Monmouth St. WC2	B41	Moxon St. W1	A39	New Inn Yd. EC2	A45
Montague Clo. SE1	A54	Mulready St. NW8	A37	New Kent Rd. SE1	A63
Montague Pl. WC1	A40	Munster Sq. NW1	B32	Newman Pass. W1	B40
Montague St. WC1	A41	Munton Rd. SE17	B63	Newmans Row WC2	B42
Montagu Ms. N. W1	A38	Muriel St. N1	A35	Newman St. W1	B40
Montagu Ms. S. W1	B38	Murphy St. SE1	A62	Newman Yd. W1	B40
Montagu Ms. W. W1	B38	Muscovy St. EC3	A55	Newnham St. E1	B45
Montagu Pl. W1	B38	Museum St. WC1	B41	Newnman Ter. SE1	A62
Montagu Sq. W1	B38	Myddelton Pass. EC1	B35	New North Pl. EC2	A44
Montagu Sq. W1	B38	Myddelton Sq. EC1	B35	New North St. WC1	A41
Montagu St. W1	B38	Myddelton St. EC1	B35	New Oxford St.	20
Montford St. EC3	B45	Mylne St. EC1	B35	New Oxford St. WC1	B40
Montpelier Ms. SW7	A58	Nash St. NW1	B32	New Palace Yd. SW1	B51
Montpelier Pl. SW7	A57	Nassau St. W1	B40	Newport Ct. WC2	A50
Montpelier Sq. SW7	A47	Neal St.	21	Newport Pl. WC2	A50
Montpelier St. SW7	A57	Neal St. WC2	B41	Newport St. SE11	B61
Montpelier Ter. SW7	A47	Neathouse Clo. SW1	A59	Newport St. WC2	A50
Montpelier Wk. SW7	A47	Nelson Sq. SE1	B53	New Quebec St. W1	B38
Montreal Pl. WC2	A51	Netley St. NW1	B33	New Row WC2	A51
Montrose Pl. SW1	B49	Neville Clo. WC1	A34	New St. Sq. EC4	B42
Monument St. EC3	A54	Neville Ct. NW8	A30	New Sq. WC2	B42
Moon St. N1	A35	Neville St. SW7	B57	New St. EC2	B45
Moore St. SW3	A58	Neville Ter. SW7	B57	Newton St. WC2	B41
Moorfields EC2	B44	New Bond St.	18	New Wharf N1	A34
Moorgate EC2	B44	New Bond St. W1	B39	Nicholas La. EC4	A54

Name	Ref	Name	Ref
Parker St. WC2	B41	Percy Cir. WC1	B35
Parkfield St. N1	A35	Percy Ms. W1	B40
Park La. W1	A48	Percy St. W1	B40
Park La. W1	B49	Percy St. WC1	B35
Park Pl. SW1	B50	Perkins Rents. SW1	A60
Park Pl. Vill. W2	A36	Perrys Pl. W1	B40
Park Rd. NW8	B30	Petersham La. SW7	A56
Park Rd. W2	B36	Petersham Ms. SW7	A56
Park Sq. E. NW1	A39	Petersham Pl. SW7	A56
Park Sq. Ms. NW1	A39	Peter's Hl. EC4	A53
Park Sq. W. NW1	A39	Peter's La. EC1	A43
Park St. SE1	A53	Peter St. W1	B40
Park St. W1	B38	Peto Pl. NW1	A39
Park Village E. NW1	A32	Petticoat La. E1	B45
Park Village W. NW1	A32	Petty France SW1	A60
Parkway NW1	A32	Petyward SW3	B57
Park West Pl. W2	B37	Philpot La. EC3	A54
Parliament Sq. SW1	B51	Phipp St. EC2	A44
Parliament St. SW1	B51	Phoenix Pl. WC1	A42
Passmore St. SW1	B58	Phoenix Rd. NW1	B33
Pastor St. SE11	B49	Phoenix St. WC2	B40
Paternoster Row EC4	B43	Piccadilly	19
Paternoster Sq. EC4	B43	Piccadilly W1	B49
Paul St. EC2	A44	Piccadilly Circus	19
Paveley St. NW8	B30	Piccadilly Cir. W1	A50
Pavilion Rd. SW1	B48	Piccadilly Pl. W1	A50
Pavilion St. SW1	A58	Pickburn Pl. EC1	A42
Peabody Av. SW1	B59	Pickering Ms. W2	B36
Peabody Bldgs. SE1	B52	Pickle Herring St. SE1	B55
Peabody Bldgs. WC1	A41	Pickwick St. SE1	B53
Peabody Est. EC1	A43	Picton Pl. W1	B39
Peabody Sq. SE1	A62	Pike Gdns. SE1	A53
Peacock St. SE17	B63	Pilgrimage St. SE1	B54
Pearman St. SE1	A62	Pilgrim St.	25
Pear Tree Ct. EC1	A42	Pilgrim St. EC4	B43
Pear Tree Ct. EC1	A43	Pilton Pl. SE17	B63
Pedley St. E1	A45	Pimlico Rd. SW1	B58
Pelham Ct. SW3	B57	Pindar St. EC2	A44
Pelham Cres. SW7	B57	Pindock Ms. W9	A36
Pelham Pl. SW7	A57	Pine St. EC1	A42
Pelham St. SW7	A57	Pit Head Ms. W1	B49
Pembroke Clo. SW1	B49	Platina St. EC2	A44
Penfold Pl. NW1	A37	Platt St. NW1	A33
Penfold St. NW8	A37	Playhouse Yd. EC4	B43
Penrhyn St. NW1	A33	Pleasant Row NW1	A32
Penrose St. SE17	B63	Plender Pl. NW1	A33
Penton Pl. SE17	B63	Plender St. NW1	A33
Penton Ri. WC1	B35	Plough Pl. EC4	B42
Penton St. N1	A35	Plough Yd. EC2	A45
Pentonville Rd. N1	B34	Plumtree Ct. EC4	B42
Pepys St. EC3	A55	Plympton St. NW8	A37
Pocock St. SE1	B53		
Poets Cor. SW1	A61		
Poland St.	19		
Poland St. W1	B40		
Pollen St. W1	B39		
Polygon Rd. NW1	B33		
Pond Ho. SW3	B57		
Pond Pl. SW3	B57		
Ponsonby Pl. SW1	B60		
Ponsonby Ter. SW1	B60		
Pont St. Ms. SW1	A58		
Pont St. SW1	A58		
Poplar Pl. W2	A46		
Poppins Ct. EC4	B42		
Porchester Gdns. W2	B36		
Porchester Gdns. Mews W2	B36		
Porchester Pl. W2	B37		
Porchester Rd. W2	B36		
Porchester Sq. W2	B36		
Porchester Ter. W2	B36		
Porchester Ter. N. W2	B36		
Porlock St. SE1	B54		
Porteus Rd. W2	A36		
Portland Pl. W1	A39		
Portman Clo. W1	B38		
Portman Ms. S. W1	B38		
Portman Sq. W1	B38		
Portman St. W1	B38		
Portpool La. EC1	A42		
Portsmouth St. WC2	B41		
Portsoken St. E1	A55		
Portugal St.	24		
Portugal St. WC2	B41		
Potter's Flds. SE1	B55		
Poultry EC2	B44		
Powis Pl. WC1	A41		
Praed Ms. W2	B37		
Praed St. W2	B37		
Pratt Wk. SE11	A61		
Prescot St. E1	A55		
Price's St. SE1	B53		
Price's Yd N1	A35		
Prideaux Pl. WC1	B35		
Primrose Hl. EC4	B42		
Primrose Hill Bridge NW8	A31		
Primrose St. EC2	A44		
Prince Albert Rd. NW1	A31		
Prince Albert Rd. NW8	B30		

Nicolson St. SE1	B53	Old Bond St. W1	A50	Osbert St. SW1	B60
Noble St. EC2	B43	Old Broad St. EC2	B44	Osborn St. E1	B45
Noel St. W1	B40	Old Burlington St. W1	A49	Oslo Ct. NW8	A30
Norfolk Cres. W2	B37	Oldbury Pl. W1	A38	Osnaburgh St. NW1	A39
Norfolk Pl. W2	B37	Old Castle St. E1	B45	Osnaburgh Ter. NW1	A39
Norfolk Rd. NW8	A29	**Old Cavendish St.**	**18**	Ossington St. W2	B35
Norfolk Row SE11	A61	Old Cavendish St. W1	B39	Ossulston St. NW1	A33
Norfolk Sq. W2	B37	Old Change Ct. EC4	A53	Osten Ms. SW7	A56
Norris St. SW1	A50	Old Church St. SW3	B57	Oswin St. SE11	A63
Northampton Bldgs. EC1	B35	Old Compton St.	**20**	Outer Circle NW1	A31
		Old Compton St. W1	B40	Outer Circle NW1	A32
Northampton Rd. EC1	A42	Old Gloucester St. WC1	A41	Outram St. NW1	A34
North Audley St. W1	B38	Old Jewry EC2	B44	Oval Rd. NW1	A32
North Bank NW8	B30	Old Marylebone Rd. NW1	B37	Ovington Gdns. SW3	A57
Northburgh St. EC1	A43			Ovington Ms. SW3	A57
North Ct. W1	A40	Old Montague St. E1	B45	Ovington Sq. SW3	A58
North Cres. WC1	A40	Old Nichol St. E2	A45	Ovington St. SW3	A58
Northdown St. N1	A34	Old North St. WC1	A41	Owens Row EC1	B35
North Gower St. NW1	B33	Old Palace Yd. SW1	A61	Owen St. EC1	B35
Northington St. WC1	A41	Old Paradise St. SE11	A61	Oxendon St. SW1	A50
North Ms. WC1	A42	Old Pk. La. W1	B49	**Oxford Circus**	**19**
North Ride W2	A47	Old Pye St. SW1	B60	Oxford Cir. W1	B39
North Row W1	B38	Old Quebec St. W1	B38	Oxford Sq. W2	B37
North Tenter St. E1	B45	Old Queen St. SW1	B50	**Oxford St.**	**18**
North Ter. SW3	A57	Old Seacoal La. EC4	B43	Oxford St. W1	B38
Northumberland All. EC3	B45	Old Sq. WC2	A42	Paddington Grn. W2	A37
Northumberland Av.	**23**	Old St. EC1	A43	Paddington St. W1	A38
Northumberland Av. WC2	A51	Olivers Yd. EC2	A44	Page St. SW1	A60
		Olympia Yd. W2	A46	Pakenham St. WC1	B35
Northumberland St. WC2	A51	O'meara St. SE1	B53	Palace Av. W8	B46
Northwest Pl. N1	A35	Omega Pl. N1	B34	Palace Gte. W8	B46
North Wharf Rd. W2	A37	Onslow Gdns. SW7	B56	Palace St. SW1	A59
Northwick Clo. NW8	B30	Onslow Ms. W. SW7	B57	Pallitt Dr. NW8	B30
Northwick Ter. NW8	B30	Onslow Sq. SW7	B57	**Pall Mall**	**22**
Norton Folgate E1	A45	Onslow St. EC1	A42	Pall Mall SW1	B50
Norwich St. EC4	B42	Ontario St. SE1	A63	**Pall Mall East**	**22**
Nott Ct. WC2	B41	Opal St. SE11	B62	Pall Mall E. SW1	A50
Nottingham Pl. W1	A38	Orange St. WC2	A50	Pall Mall Pl. SW1	A50
Nottingham St. W1	A38	Orchardson St. NW8	A37	Palmer St. SW1	A60
Nutford Pl. W1	B38	Orchard St. W1	B38	Pancras La. EC4	B44
Oakden St. SE11	B62	Orde Hall St. WC1	A41	Pancras Rd. NW1	A33
Oakley Sq. NW1	A33	Ordnance Hl. NW8	A30	**Panton St.**	**20**
Oak Tree Rd. NW8	B30	Orient St. SE11	A62	Panton St. SW1	A50
Oat La. EC2	B43	Orme La. W2	A46	Panyer Alley EC4	B43
Occupation Rd. SE17	B63	Orme Sq. W2	A46	Pardon St. EC1	A43
Ogle St. W1	A40	Ormonde Gte. SW3	B58	Paris Gdn. SE1	A52
Old Bailey EC4	B43	Ormonde Ter. NW8	A31	Park Clo. SW1	B48
Old Barrack Yd. SW1	B48	Ormond Ms. WC1	A41	Park Cres. W1	A39
Old Bond St.	**19**	Ormond Yd. SW1	A50	Park Cres. Ms. E. W1	A39
		Orsett St. SE11	B61	Park Cres. Ms. W. W1	A39
		Orsett Ter. W2	B36	Parkers Row SE1	B55

Theobald's Rd. WC1	A41	Tower St. WC2	B41	Upr. Grosvenor St. W1	A48
Theobald's Rd. WC1	A42	Townley St. SE17	B63	Upr. Ground SE1	B52
Thirleby Rd. SW1	A60	Townsend Est. NW8	A30	Upr. Harley St. NW1	A39
Thistle Gro. SW10	B56	Townshend Rd. NW8	A30	Upr. James St. W1	A50
Thomas Doyle St. SE1	A63	Toynbee St. E1	B45	Upr. John St. W1	A50
Thomas Moore St. E1	A55	Tracey St. SE11	B62	Upr. Marsh SE1	B62
Thorney St. SW1	A61	Trafalgar Sq.	22	Upr. Montague St. W1	A38
Thornhaugh St. WC1	A41	Trafalgar Sq. WC2	A51	Upr. St. Martin's La.	A51
Thornton Pl. W1	A38	Transept St. NW1	A37	WC2	
Thorpe St. E1	B45	Treaty St. N1	A34	Upper St. N1	A35
Thrale St. SE1	B53	Trebeck St. W1	A49	Upr. Thames St. EC4	B44
Thrawl St. E1	B45	Tregunter Rd. SW10	B56	Upr. Wimpole St. W1	A39
Threadneedle St. EC2	B44	Tresham Cres. NW8	B30		
Three Kings Yd. W1	A49	Treveris St. SE1	B53	Valentine Pl. SE1	B52
Three Oak La. SE1	B55	Trevor Pl. SW7	B47	Valentine's Row SE1	B52
Throgmorton Av. EC2	B44	Trevor Sq. SW7	B48	Vandon Pass. SW1	A60
Throgmorton St. EC2	B44	Trevor St. SW7	B48	Vandon St. SW1	A60
Thrush St. SE17	B63	Trinity Church Sq. SE1	A63	Vandy St. EC2	A44
Thurloe Clo. SW7	A57	Trinity Sq. EC3	A55	Vane St. SW1	A60
Thurloe Pl. SW7	A57	Trinity St. SE1	A63	Varndell St. NW1	B32
Thurloe Pl. Ms. SW7	A57	Trio Pl. SE1	A63	Vauxhall Bri. Rd. SW1	A59
Thurloe Sq. SW7	A57	Triton Sq. NW1	B33	Vauxhall Gdns. Est.	B61
Thurloe St. SW7	A57	Trump St. EC2	B43	SE11	
Thurlow Ct. SW3	B57	Trundle St. SE1	B53	Vauxhall St. SE11	B61
Tichborne Row W2	B37	Tryon St. SW3	B58	Vauxhall Wk. SE11	B61
Tilney St. W1	A49	Tudor St.	25	Venables St. NW8	A37
Timber St. EC1	A43	Tudor St. EC4	A52	Vere St. W1	B39
Tinworth Ho. SE11	B61	Tufton St. SW1	A61	Vernon Pl. WC1	B41
Tinworth St. SE11	B61	Turks Head Yard EC1	A42	Vernon Ri. WC1	B35
Titchfield Rd. NW8	A31	Turks Row SW3	B58	Vernon Sq. WC1	B35
Tite St. SW3	B58	Turnmill St. EC1	A42	Verulam Bldgs. WC1	A42
Tiverton St. SE1	A63	Turpentine La. SW1	A59	Verulam St. WC1	A42
Token Ho. Yd. EC2	B44	Turquand St. SE17	B63	Viceroy Ct. NW8	A31
Tolmers Sq. WC1	B33	Turve St. E2	A45	Victoria Av.	B45
Tonbridge St. WC1	B34	Twyford St. N1	A34	Victoria Embankment	23
Took's Ct. EC4	B42	Twyford St. WC2	B41	Victoria Emb. SE1	B51
Tooley St. SE1	B54	Tybalds Est. WC1	A41	Victoria Emb. WC2	A51
Tooley St. SE1	B55	Tyburn Way W1	B38	Victoria Rd. W8	A56
Topaz St. SE11	B62	Tyer's Est. SE1	B54	Victoria Sq. SW1	A59
Topham St. EC1	A42	Tyer's Gte. SE1	B54	Victoria St. SW1	A59
Torrens St. EC1	A35	Tyers St. SE11	B61	Victory Pl. SE17	B63
Torrington Pl. WC1	A40	Tyers Ter. SE11	B61	Vigo St.	19
Tothill St. SW1	A60	Tysoe St. EC1	B35	Vigo St. W1	A50
Tottenham Court Rd.	20	Udall St. SW1	B60	Villiers St.	23
Tottenham Ct. Rd. W1	A40	Ufford St. SE1	B52	Villiers St. WC2	A51
Tottenham St. W1	A40	Union St. SE1	B53	Vincent Sq. SW1	B60
Toulmin St. SE1	B53	University St. WC1	A40	Vincent St. SW1	B60
Tower Bridge Northern		Upbrook Ms. W2	B36	Vine Hl. EC1	B35
App. E1		Upr. Belgrave St. SW1	A59	Vine La. SE1	B54
Tower Hl. EC3	A55	Upr. Berkeley St. W1	B38	Vinery Vill. NW8	B30
Tower Pl. EC3	A55	Upr. Brook St. W1	A48	Vine St. EC3	B45

Vine St. Bri. EC1	A42	
Vine Yd. SE1	B53	
Viney Wk. EC1	A42	
Vintners Pl. EC4	A53	
Virgil St. SE1	A62	
Viscount St. EC1	A43	
Wadding St. SE17	A63	
Waithman St. EC4	B43	
Wakefield St. WC1	B34	
Walbrook EC4	A54	
Walcorde Av. SE17	B63	
Walcot Sq. SE11	A62	
Walker Ho. NW1	B33	
Walkers Ct. W1	B40	
Walnut Tree Wk. SE11	A62	
Walpole St. SW3	B58	
Walton Pl. SW3	A58	
Walton St. SW3	A57	
Walworth Rd. SE17	B63	
Wansey St. SE17	B63	
Wardens Grn. SE1	B63	
Wardour Ms. W1	B40	
Wardour St.	**19**	
Wardour St. W1	B40	
Wardour St. W1	A50	
Warner St. EC1	A42	
Warren St. W1	A39	
Warrington Cres. W9	A36	
Warwick Av. W9	A36	
Warwick Ct. WC1	B42	
Warwick Cres. W2	A36	
Warwick Est. W2	A36	
Warwick Ho. St. SW1	A50	
Warwick La. EC4	B43	
Warwick Pl. SW1	B59	
Warwick Pl. W9	A36	
Warwick Row SW1	A59	
Warwick Sq. EC4	B43	
Warwick Sq. SW1	B59	
Warwick Sq. Ms. SW1	B59	
Warwick St. W1	A50	
Warwick Way SW1	B59	
Warwick Yd. EC1	A43	
Watergate EC4	A52	
Watergate Wk. WC2	A51	
Waterloo Bri.	**24**	
Waterloo Pl.	**22**	
Waterloo Pl. SW1	A50	
Waterloo Rd. SE1	A52	
Water St. WC2	A52	
Watling St. EC4	B43	
Waverley Pl. NW8	A30	
Waverton St. W1	A49	
Weavers La. SE1	B55	
Weaver St. E1	A45	
Webber Row SE1	B52	
Webber St. SE1	B52	
Weighho St. W1	B39	
Weirs Pass. NW1	B33	
Welbeck St.	**18**	
Welbeck St. W1	B39	
Welbeck Way W1	B39	
Wellers Cres. NW1	A34	
Weller St. SE1	B53	
Wellington Arch W1	B49	
Wellington Ct. NW8	A30	
Wellington Pl. NW8	B30	
Wellington Rd. NW8	A30	
Wellington Sq. SW3	B58	
Wellington St.	**21**	
Wellington St. WC2	A51	
Wells Ms. W1	B40	
Wells Ri. NW8	A31	
Wells Sq.	B35	
Wells St.	**19**	
Wells St. W1	B40	
Welsey Clo. SE17	B63	
Wenworth St. E1	B45	
Werrington St. NW1	A33	
Wesley St. W1	A39	
Westbourne Bri. W2	A36	
Westbourne Cres. W2	B37	
Westbourne Gdns. W2	B36	
Westbourne Gro. Ter. W2	B36	
Westbourne Ms. W2	B36	
Westbourne Pk. Ms. W2	B36	
Westbourne St. W2	B37	
Westbourne Ter. W2	B36	
Westbourne Ter. Rd. W2	A36	
West Central Pl. WC1	B41	
West Eaton Pl. SW1	A58	
Westgate Ter. SW10	B56	
West Halkin St. SW1	A58	
West Harding St. EC4	B42	
Westminster Bri. Rd. SE1	B52	
Westmoreland Bldgs. EC1	B43	
Westmoreland Pl. SW1	B59	
Westmoreland St. W1	A39	
Westmoreland Ter. SW1	B59	
Weston Ri. WC1	B34	
Weston St. SE1	B54	
West Poultry Av. EC1	B43	
West Smithfield EC1	B43	
West Sq. SE11	A62	
West St.	**20**	
West St. EC2	B44	
West St. WC2	B41	
West Tenter St. E1	B45	
West Warwick Pl. SW1	B59	
Wetherby Gdns. SW5	B56	
Wetherby Ms. SW5	B56	
Wetherby Pl. SW7	B56	
Weymouth Ms. W1	A39	
Weymouth St. W1	A39	
Wharfdale Rd. N1	A34	
Wharf Rd. NW1	A34	
Wharfside EC4	A54	
Wharton St. WC1	B35	
Wheat St. W1	A39	
Wheler St. E1	A45	
Whetstone Pk. WC2	B41	
Whidborne St. WC1	B34	
Whiskin St. EC1	B35	
Whitby St. E1	A45	
Whitcomb St.	**22**	
Whitcomb St. WC2	A50	
Whitechapel High St. E1	B45	
Whitechapel Rd. E1	B45	
White Church La. E1	B45	
White Conduit St. N1	A35	
Whitecross Pl. EC2	A44	
Whitecross St. EC1	A43	
Whitefriars St. EC4	B42	
Whitehall	**23**	
Whitehall SW1	B51	
Whitehall Ct.	**23**	
Whitehall Ct. SW1	B51	
Whitehall Gdns. SW1	B51	
Whitehall Pl.	**23**	
Whitehall Pl. SW1	B51	
White Hart St. SE11	B62	
White Hart Yd. SE1	B54	
Whitehaven St. NW8	A37	

Whiteheads Gro. SW3	B57	Wilson St. EC2	B44	Woodseer St. E1	A45
Whitehorse St. W1	B49	Wilton Cres. SW1	B48	Woods Ms. W1	A48
White Kennet St. E1	B45	Wilton Ms. SW1	A59	Woodstock Ms. W1	A39
White Lion St. N1	A35	Wilton Pl. SW1	B48	Woodstock St. W1	B39
Whites Grounds SE1	B54	Wilton Rd. SW1	A59	Wood St. EC2	B43
White's Grounds Est. SE1	B54	Wilton Row SW1	B48	Wootton St. SE1	B52
		Wilton St. SW1	A59	Worgan St. SE11	B61
White's Row E1	B45	Wilton Ter. SW1	B58	Wormwood St. EC2	B44
Whitfield Pl. W1	A40	Wiltshire Clo. SW3	B58	Woronzow Rd. NW8	A30
Whitfield St. W1	A40	Wimpole Ms. W1	A39	Worship St. EC2	A44
Whitgift St. SE11	B61	**Wimpole St.**	**18**	Wren St. WC1	A42
Whittaker St. SW1	B58	Wimpole St. W1	A39	Wyndham Ms. W1	A38
Whittlesey St. SE1	B52	Winchester Clo. SE17	B63	Wyndham Pl. W1	A38
Wickham St. SE11	B61	Winchester Sq. SE1	A54	Wyndham St. W1	A38
Wicklow St. WC1	B34	Winchester St. SE1	A54	Wynford Rd. N1	A35
Wide Gates E1	B45	Winchester St. SW1	A59	Wynyard Ter. SE11	B62
Wigmore Pl. W1	B39	Winchester Wk. SE1	B54	Wythburn Pl. W1	B38
Wigmore St.	**18**	Wincott St. SE11	B62	Yardley St. WC1	B35
Wigmore St. W1	B38	**Windmill St.**	**20**	Yarmouth Pl. W1	B49
Wilbraham Pl. SW1	A58	Windmill St. W1	B40	Yeomans Row SW3	A57
Wild Ct. WC2	B41	Windmill St. W1	A50	York Av.	B63
Wild St. WC2	B41	Windmill Wk. SE1	B52	York Bridge NW1	A38
Wilfred St. SW1	A60	Windsor Pl. SW1	A60	York Bldgs. WC2	A51
Wilkes St.	A45	**Wine Office Ct.**	**25**	York Gte. NW1	A39
William Ms. SW1	B48	Wine Office Ct. EC4	B42	York Pl. WC2	A51
William Rd. NW1	B32	Winsland Ms. W2	B37	York Rd. SE1	B51
William St. SW1	B48	Winsland St. W2	B37	York St. W1	A38
William IV St.	**21**	Winsley St. W1	B40	York Ter. E. NW1	A39
William IV St. WC2	A51	Withers Pl. EC1	A43	York Ter. W. NW1	A38
Willow Pl. SW1	A60	Woburn Pl. WC1	A41	York Way N1	A34
Willow St. EC2	A44	Woburn Sq. WC1	A40	York Way Ct. N1	A34
Willy St. WC1	B41	Woburn Wk. WC1	B33	Young St. W8	B46
Wilmington Sq. WC1	B35	Wolseley St. SE1	B55	Zoar St.	A53
Wilmington St. WC1	B35	Woodbridge St. EC1	A42		
		Woodfall St. SW3	B58		

NOTES

NOTES

NOTES